Judgement-Proof Robots and Artificial Intelligence

Mitja Kovač

Judgement-Proof Robots and Artificial Intelligence

A Comparative Law and Economics Approach

palgrave
macmillan

Mitja Kovač
School of Economics and Business
University of Ljubljana
Ljubljana, Slovenia

ISBN 978-3-030-53643-5 ISBN 978-3-030-53644-2 (eBook)
https://doi.org/10.1007/978-3-030-53644-2

This Palgrave Macmillan imprint is published by the registered company Springer Nature Switzerland AG
The registered company address is: Gewerbestrasse 11, 6330 Cham, Switzerland

Preface

This book is about the future of unimaginable progress where the wildest dreams of visionary scientists materialized. It is about a futuristic world in which super-intelligent, superhuman artificial intelligence serves as human compatible and, among other things, acts in its own will. It is also about unprecedented and currently uncontemplated hazards that such superhuman and super-intelligent artificial intelligence may impose on human societies. However, this book is not about a super-intelligent AI that is conscious, since no one working in the AI field is attempting to make machines conscious. Famous Hollywood movies like "I robot" where a god detective Spooner—alias Will Smith—chases hordes of evil and conscious robots attempting to enslave humans are actually missing the point. It is competence, and not consciousness, that matters. Namely, if one writes an algorithm that when running will form and carry out a plan which will result in significant damages to life or property, unforeseeable hazards or even in the destruction of a human race, then it is not about the AI's consciousness but about its competence and capacity.

Of course, no one can predict exactly how the AI will develop but undoubtedly it will be the dominant technology of the future. Nevertheless, policymakers and lawmakers must prepare *ex ante* for the possibility that AI will become super-intelligent and that its actions might cause severe damages and hazards. This book is thus an attempt to provide a law and economics treatment of such uncontemplated development and should be regarded as a contribution to lawmakers and legal practitioners around the world to learn how to avoid the risks, mitigate potential hazards and to offer a set of regulatory tools that could be employed in *ex ante* controlling, regulating the potentially biggest event in human history.

This book could not have been made without the enthusiastic support of my parents and my loved ones.

My special gratitude goes also to Professor Gerrit De Geest from Washington University in St. Louis for his extraordinary, fascinating, inspiring, and path-breaking discussions and lectures which I have been privileged to follow and admire.

I am especially indebted to and would like to express our sincere gratitude for their precious substantive comments, insights, reflections, feedbacks, suggestions, discussions, and inspiration to: Paul Aubrecht, Nick van der Beek, Roger van den Bergh, John Bell, Greta Bosch, Boudewijn Bouckaert, Marianne Breier, Miriam Buiten, Giuseppe Dari-Mattiachi, Gerrit De Geest, Ben Depoorter, Larry DiMatteo, Thomas Eger, Jan Essink, Michael Faure, Luigi Franzoni, Nuno Garupa, Paula Giliker, Victor Goldberg, James Gordley, Alice Guerra, Eric Helland, Johan den Hertog Sven Hoeppner, Roland Kirstein, Jonathan Klick, Anne Lafarre, Henrik Lando, Igor Loncarski, Anthony Ogus, Vernon Palmer, Francesco Parisi, Alessio Pacces, Catherine Pedamon, Roy Pertain, Christina Poncibo, Jens Prüffer, Elena Reznichenko, Wolf-Georg Ringe, Hans-Bernd Schäfer, Matej Marinc, Marcus Smith, Dusan Mramor, Nancy Van Nuffel, Holger Spamann, Rok Spruk, Christoph Van der Elst, Ann-Sophie Vandenberghe, Stefan Voight, Franziska Weber, Wicher Schreuders, Louis Visscher, Spela Vizjak, Elisabeth Wielinger, and Wolfgang Weigel.

I am also grateful to Miha Škerlevaj, Sandra Durašević, Martina Petan, Ivana Pranjić, Dunja Zlotrg, Erna Emrić, Tadeja Žabkar, Rebeka Koncilja, and Vesna Žabkar for their daily, round-a-clock care and immense organizational support. This is also the place to thank the publisher Palgrave Macmillan on behalf of all contributing authors in particular to Ruth Jenner, Arun Kumar and Ruth Noble as the responsible publisher officers.

I could not have completed this book without the support of Slovenian Research Agency (*Agencija za raziskovalno dejavnost Republike Slovenije*), since this book is part of our project "Challenges of inclusive sustainable development in the predominant paradigm of economic and business sciences" (P5-0128).

Finally, thanks are due to my Dean Professor Metka Tekavčič (School of Economics and Business University of Ljubljana) and to all of my colleagues from the University of Ljubljana.

This book has been written in the times of stress when the Covid-19 pandemic locked down the entire European continent. The project itself has been, during my teaching visits at the Erasmus University of Rotterdam and at the Ghent University, gradually developed over the past three years. I do hope that you will enjoy it.

Ljubljana, Slovenia
Ghent, Belgium
Rotterdam, The Netherlands
May 2020

Mitja Kovač

Contents

About the Author

Mitja Kovač was born in 1976, graduated law with "cum laude" at the University of Ljubljana, Faculty of Law (Slovenia). He gained his LL.M. and Ph.D. in the field of comparative contract law and economics at Utrecht University, Faculty of Law, Economics and Governance (The Netherlands). In 2006 he became also a member of the Economic Impact Group within the CoPECL Network of Excellence (European DCFR project). He was a visiting professor at the ISM University of Management and Economics in Vilnius (Lithuania) and a research fellow at the British Institute of International and Comparative Law in London (UK) and at Washington University School of Law in St. Louis (USA). Currently, he is an associate professor at the University of Ljubljana, School of Economics and Business (Slovenia), a visiting lecturer at the Erasmus University Rotterdam (The Netherlands), at University of Ghent (Belgium), at the University of Turin (Italy), and at University of Vienna (Austria). He publishes in the fields of comparative contract law and economics, new institutional economics, consumer protection, contract theory, and competition law and economics.

His papers appear in the *Journal of Institutional Economics*, *Economics & Politics*, *Journal of Regulatory Economics*, *Swiss Journal of Economics and Statistics*, *International Review of Law and Economics*, *European Journal of Risk Regulation*, *Asian Journal of Law and Economics*, *Journal of Comparative Law*, *Maastricht Journal of European and Comparative Law*, *Business Law Review*, *European Review of Contract Law*, *European*

Review of Private Law, *Journal of Consumer Policy*, *European Journal of Comparative Law and Governance*, and *Global Journal of Comparative Law* and his books on comparative contract law and economics and on the economic evidence in the EU competition law are published by Edward Elgar, Kluwer, and Intersentia publishers. Moreover, his paper (co-authored with Amira Elkanawati, Vita Gjikolli, and Ann-Sophie Vandenberghe) on "The Covid-19 Pandemic: Collective Action and European Public Policy" was in April 2020 listed on SSRN's Top Ten download list for the fields of international institutions, European political economy, and public choice.

He sings as a second tenor in the Vocal Academy of Ljubljana male chamber choir (*Grand Prix Citta e Di Arezzo 2009* and *Grand Prix Europe 2010* awards) and was a member of the Croatian offshore sailing team on its sailing expedition around the world (*Čigrom oko svijeta*).

Reviewers

Prof. Dr. Alessio M. Pacces (University of Amsterdam), and
As. Prof. Dr. Sven Hoeppner (Otto-von-Guericke-University of Magdeburg).

Abbreviations

AGI	Artificial General Intelligence
AI	Artificial Intelligence
ASI	Artificial Specific Intelligence
BGB	Bürgerliches Gesetz Buch
CAV	Connected and Autonomous Vehicle
CNN	Convolutional Neural Network
DART	Dynamic Analysis and Replanning Tool
DL	Deep Learning
EU	European Union
HMM	Hidden Markov model
IA	Intelligent Automation
LISP	High-Level Programming Language
MIT	Massachusetts Institute of Technology
ML	Machine Learning
SNARC	Stochastic Neural Analog Reinforcement Calculator
UN	United Nations

CHAPTER 1

Introduction

Abstract The introduction summarizes a book outline, introduces individual chapters, and discusses some of the main concepts used.

Keywords Law and economics · Regulation · Autonomous artificial systems · Judgement-proof problem

Artificial intelligence and its recent breakthroughs in the machine–human interactions and machine learning technology are increasingly affecting almost every sphere of our lives. It is on an exponential curve and some of its materializations represent an increased privacy threat (Kosinski and Yilun 2018), might be ethically questionable (e.g. child-sex bots), and even potentially dangerous and harmful (e.g. accidents caused by autonomous self-driving vehicles, ships, and planes or autonomous decision to kill by machines). Big data economies, robotization, autonomous artificial intelligence, and their impact on societies have recently received increasing scholarly attention in economics, law, sociology, philosophy, and natural sciences.

Superfast economic changes spurred by worldwidely integrated markets, creation of artificial intelligence and related explosive gathering and processing of unimaginable large data (big data) by the artificial intelligence represent one of the most triggering questions of the modern world. One that can even rival the fatal issue of the global climate change.

M. Kovač, *Judgement-Proof Robots and Artificial Intelligence*,
https://doi.org/10.1007/978-3-030-53644-2_1

Namely, the artificial intelligence is undoubtedly unleashing a new industrial revolution and, in order to govern the currently uncontemplated hazards, it is of vital importance for the lawmakers around the globe to address its systemic challenges and regulate its economic and social effects without stifling innovation.

The founding father of modern computer science and artificial intelligence Alan Turing envisaged such a trajectory and, in a lecture, given in Manchester in 1951 considered the subjugation of humankind:

> It seems probable that once the machine thinking method had started, it would not take long to outstrip our feeble powers. There would be no question of the machines dying, and they would be able to converse with each other to sharpen their wits. At some stage therefore we should have to expect the machines to take control, in the way that is mentioned in Samuel Butler's *Erewhom*. (Turing 1951)

More recently Russell (2019) argues that technical community has suffered from a failure of imagination when discussing the nature and impact of super-intelligent AI. Russell (2019) suggests that often we see "discussions of reduced medical errors, safer cars or other advances of an incremental nature." He also advances that:

> ...robots are imagined as individual entities carrying their brains with them, whereas in fact they are likely to be wirelessly connected into a single, global entity that draws on vast stationary computing resources. It is if researchers are afraid of examining the real consequences of AI A general-purpose intelligent system can, by assumption, do what any human can do. (Russell 2019)

Current trends that lean towards developing autonomous machines, with the capacity to interact, learn, and take autonomous decisions, indeed hold a variety of concerns regarding their direct and indirect effect that call for a substantive law and economics treatment. The super-intelligent artificial intelligence will, as I argue throughout this book, also change immensely the entire institutional and conceptual structure of the law. Super-influencer and industrial visionary Elon Musk for example advocates an urgent legislative action that would regulate globally the artificial intelligence before it will be too late. At the U.S. National Governors Association 2017 summer meeting in Providence, Musk famously stated that "the US government's current framework for regulation would be dangerous with artificial intelligence because of the existential risk it poses to humanity (Gibbs 2017)." Moreover, Musk sees artificial intelligence as the "most serious threat to the survival of human race" (Gibbs 2017). Policymakers around the world have been actually urged to address the growing legal vacuum in virtually every domain affected by technological advancement.

However, normally, the way regulations are set up is when a bunch of bad things happen, there's a public outcry, and after many years a regulatory agency is set up to regulate that industry. This book seeks to address this problem of the reflective regulatory action, where a bunch of bad things need to happen to trigger the regulatory response and urges for a pre-emptive, *ex ante* regulatory approach where actions are taken before bad things happen and before there is a public outcry. There is a simple reason for such an approach. Namely, as Musk suggests, the absence of such a pre-emptive regulatory action might indeed be a fatal one.

Meanwhile, Europeans, lagging slightly behind the artificial intelligence's technological breakthrough of the United States and China, have not come to grips with what is ethical, let alone with what the law should be and result is a growing legal vacuum in almost every domain affected by this unprecedented technological development. For example, European lawyers are currently passionately discussing what happens when a self-driving car has a software failure and hits pedestrian, or a drone's camera happens to catch someone skinny-dipping in a pool or taking a shower, or a robot kills a human in a self-defence? Is then the manufacturer or the maker of the software or the owner or the user or even the autonomous artificial intelligence himself responsible if something goes wrong?

Having regard to these developments European Parliament already in 2017 adopted a Resolution on the Civil Law Rules on Robotics (P8-TA (2017)0051) and requested the EU Commission to submit on the basis of Article 114 TFEU, a proposal for a directive on civil law rules and to consider the designation of a European Agency for Robotics and Artificial Intelligence in order to provide the technical, ethical, and regulatory expertise. EU Parliament also proposed a code of ethical conduct for robotics engineers a code for research ethics committees, a licence for designers, and a licence for users.

Moreover, lawmakers around the world and particularly the EU Commission also consider that the civil liability for damage caused by the robots (and any form of artificial intelligence) is a crucial issue which also needs to be analysed and addressed at the Union level in order to ensure efficiency, transparency, and consistency in the implementation of legal certainty throughout the EU. In other words, lawmakers wonder whether strict liability or the risk management approach (obligatory insurance or a special compensation fund) should be applied in instances where artificial intelligence causes damage. Furthermore, stakeholders also debate whether an autonomous artificial intelligence should be characterized in the existing legal categories or whether for example a new category with specific rules should be created? If lawmakers would indeed embark on such a journey and proceed with an establishment of such a separate legal entity, then the triggering question is what kind of category shall we have?

As an illustration, consider the current rules on the European continent where autonomous artificial intelligence cannot be held liable per se for actors or omissions that cause damage, since it may not be possible to identify the party responsible for providing compensation and to require that party to make good the damage it has caused (Erdelyi and Goldsmith 2018; Breland 2017; Wadhwa 2014). Current Directive 85/374/EEC adopted more than thirty years ago covers merely damage caused by artificial intelligence's manufacturing defects and on condition that the injured person is able to prove the actual damage, the defect in the product, and the causal relationship between damage and defect. Therefore, strict liability or liability without fault may not be sufficient to induce the optimal precaution and internalization of risks. Namely, the new super-intelligent artificial intelligence generation will sooner or later be capable of autonomously learning from their own variable experience and will interact with their environment in a unique and unforeseeable manner. Such autonomous, self-learning, decision-making autonomous super-intelligence might then present a substantive limitation to the deterrence and prevention effects and related incentive streams of current regulatory framework.

Regarding the question of strict liability, the law and economics scholarship has witnessed the transformation of product liability, from simple negligence to the far more complex concept of strict product liability (Schäfer and Ott 2004; Kraakman 2000). This change has been triumphed by many as a victory for consumers and safer products. However, scholars found that the reverse occurred (Herbig and Golden 1994; Malott 1988; McGuire 2016). Literature also shows that product liability costs in the United States have prompted some manufacturers to abandon valuable new technologies, life-saving drugs, and innovative product designs (Herbig and Golden 1994; Malott 1988; McGuire 2016). Thus, traditional law and economics scholarship suggests that very strict tort law regimes might indeed stifle the artificial intelligence innovation and hence it might be inappropriate policy respond.

This book complements my earlier work (Kovac 2020) and seeks to address the role of public policy in regulating the superhuman artificial intelligence and related civil liability for damage caused by such superhuman artificial intelligence. Such superhuman artificial intelligence may (though this right now may still sound as a futuristic or science-fiction scenario) in the near future cause uncontemplated hazards and harm to humans but will not be able to make victims whole for the harm incurred and might not have incentives (autonomous AI might simply not care about the caused harm) for safety efforts created by standard tort law enforced through monetary sanctions. These phenomena are known in the law and economics literature as a "judgement-proof problem." This "judgement-proof problem" is a standard argument in lawmaking discussions operationalizing policies, doctrines, and the rules. A person or a thing is "judgement-proof" when she is financially insolvent, or whose income and assets cannot be obtained in satisfaction of a judgement. Throughout this book we will employ a broad judgement-proof definition to include also a problem of dilution of incentives to reduce risk which materializes due to person's complete indifference to the *ex ante* possibility of being found liable by the legal system for harms done to others and complete indifference to the potential accident liability (the value of expected sanction equals zero).

This problem of dilution of incentives (broad judgement-proof definition) is distinct from the problem that scholars and practitioners usually perceive as a "judgement-proof problem" which is generally identified with injurer's inability to pay fully for losses and victims' inability to obtain complete compensation (Huberman et al. 1983; Keeton and Kwerel 1984). Thus, in this book we employ a broad definition of a judgement-proof problem which encompasses all potential sources of dilution of incentives to reduce risk and not merely the narrow tortfeasor's inability to pay for the damages. Identified judgement-proof characteristics of super-intelligent AI agent might, as this book seeks to show, completely undermine the deterrence and insurance goals of private law and tort law and result in excessive levels of harm and unprecedented hazards.

The traditional law and economics literature on the classic human-related judgement-proof problem is vast and has been exploring effects, extent, and potential remedies to this unwelcome disturbance in the liability system (Ganuza and Gomez 2005; Boyd and Ingberman 1994). However, the extrapolation of this classic concept upon the features of the autonomous artificial intelligence has, at least to my knowledge, not been made yet and represents one of the essential contributions of this book.

This law and economics concept has been coined in 1986 by Professor Steven Shavell in his seminal article on the "judgement-proof problem." While employing law and economics insights of the judgement-proof problem (Shavell 1986) upon artificial intelligence and machine learning technologies book offers several, economically inspired, instrumental insights for an improved liability law regime and offers a set of recommendations for an improved, worldwide regulatory intervention which should deter hazardous enterprises, induce optimal precaution and simultaneously preserve dynamic efficiency—incentives to innovate undistorted. Namely, technological progress increases productivity and expands the range of products available to consumers, and has historically been the root of sustained economic growth (Acemoglu and Robinson 2019; Acemoglu and Zilibotti 2001; Acemoglu 1997). The potential efficiency gains that the autonomous artificial intelligence may offer to our societies are simply significant and hence should not be deterred. What is needed, however, is a fine-tuning of the balance between the progress and dynamic efficiency on one side and on the other the *ex ante* prevention of potential hazards.

The potential independent development and self-learning capacity of a super-intelligent AI agent might cause its de facto immunity from tort law's deterrence capacity and consequential externalization of the precaution costs. Moreover, the prospect that superhuman AI agent might behave in ways designers or manufacturers did not expect (as shown in the previous chapter this might be a very realistic scenario) challenges the prevailing assumption within human-related tort law that courts only compensate for foreseeable injuries. The chances are that if we manage to build super-intelligent AI agent with any degree of autonomy our legal system will be unprepared and unable to control them.

This book is divided into two parts. Part I offers a conceptual framework and deals with the law and economics methodology, discusses the optimal regulatory intervention framework, and introduces the main, unique features of the autonomous artificial intelligence; whereas Part II offers discussions on negligence, strict and product liability, judgement-proof problem, optimal regulatory timing, and an improved liability law regime.

Chapter 2 offers a synthesis of the employed law and economics methodology and provides an overview of the concepts of rationality, risk-aversion, transaction cost phenomena, and investigates the nature of economic reasoning. The chapter also offers a brief historical narrative of the employed methodology and investigates the relationship between the positive and normative analysis. Moreover, this chapter also provides a brief summary of the notion of behavioural law and economics and offers a general implication and evidences of non-rational behaviour.

Chapter 3 of this book deals with the context of regulation and discusses the nature of regulation, theories of regulation and embodied economic reasoning, scope and forms of regulation, and historical development of regulation in the EU. It introduces the concepts of perfect markets, market failures and related nature, and scope and form of regulation. In addition, it introduces the reader with the concepts of cooperation, third-party effects, economic and non-economic goals of regulation, and sets the framework for an optimal level of regulatory activity.

In Chapter 4 an introduction to the autonomous artificial intelligence systems is presented. This chapter discusses the origins of the autonomous AI, offers definitions, introduces the concepts of super-intelligence, deep learning, machine learning, uncertainty, reasoning, robotics, and causation. In addition, it critically examines the relationship between big data and autonomous AI, between automated bias and discrimination, and related market distorting effects. Moreover, this chapter explores the unique design features of autonomous AI, discusses the notion of agents with common sense, robust learning, reinforcement learning, grounding, robot learning in homes, intuitive physics, and triggering issue of embodied agents. This chapter attempts to explain the main concepts, definitions and developments of the field of artificial intelligence. It addresses the issues of logic, probability, perception, learning, and action. The chapter examines the current "state of the art" of the artificial intelligent systems and its recent developments.

Part II of this book deals with the judgement-proof problem and the autonomous AI. In the first chapter, Chapter 5, it is argued that the newest generation of super-intelligent AI agents learn to gang up and cooperate against humans, without communicating or being told to do so. Sophisticated autonomous AI agents even collude to raise prices instead of competing to create better deals and they do decide to gouge their customers and humans. This chapter also shows that super-intelligent AI systems might be used towards undesirable ends, the use of AI systems might result in a loss of accountability and the ultimate, unregulated success of AI might mean the end of the human race. Moreover, this chapter suggests that the main issue related to the super-intelligent AI is not their consciousness but rather their competence to cause harm and hazards.

Chapter 6 identifies the "judgement-proof problem" as a standard argument in lawmaking discussions operationalizing policies, doctrines, and the rules. This chapter suggests that a super-intelligent AI agent may cause harm to others but will due to judgement-proofness not be able to make victims whole for the harm incurred and might not have incentives for safety efforts created by standard tort law enforced through monetary sanctions. Moreover, this chapter also argues that the potential independent development and self-learning capacity of a super-intelligent AI agent might cause its de facto immunity from tort law's deterrence capacity and consequential externalization of the precaution costs. Furthermore, the chapter shows that the prospect that a super-human AI agent might behave in ways designers or manufacturers did not expect (as shown in the previous chapter this might be a very realistic scenario) challenges the prevailing assumption within tort law that courts only compensate for foreseeable injuries.

The next chapter deals with the fundamental legal concepts and regulatory key questions. In Chapter 7 the issues of autonomous AI and moral choices, systematic underestimation of risks, use of force, liability, safety, and certification are addressed. This chapter also investigates key policy initiatives and offers a substantive analysis of the optimal regulatory intervention. It discusses the concepts of regulatory sandboxes, negligence, strict and product liability, vicarious liability, accident compensation schemes, insurance and the tort law, and economic insights of the judgement-proof problem. Moreover, it offers a critical examination of separate legal personality, robot rights, and offers a set of arguments for an optimal regulatory intervention and for an optimal regulatory timing. In addition, this chapter provides economically inspired, instrumental insights for an improved liability law regime, strict liability, and principal–agent relationships.

To end, there is an attempt at an anti-fragile view of the law and its persistent, robust responses to uncontemplated technological shocks and related hazards. Namely, law might be much more resilient in dealing with technological innovation and related hazards than it is often believed. This feature of the legal system in allowing it to deal with the unknown is beyond resilience and robustness, since every technological shock in the last millennium actually made the legal system even better.

Bibliography

Acemoglu, Daron, and James A. Robinson. 2019. *The Narrow Corridor: States, Societies, and the Fate of Liberty*. New York: Penguin Press.

Acemoglu, Daron, and Fabrizio Zilibotti. 2001. Productivity Differences. *The Quarterly Journal of Economics* 116 (2): 563–606.

Acemoglu, Daron. 1997. Technology, Unemployment and Efficiency. *European Economic Review* 41 (3–5): 525–533.

Boyd, James, and Daniel E. Ingberman. 1994. Noncompensatory Damages and Potential Insolvency. *Journal of Legal Studies* 23 (2): 895–910.

Breland, Ali. 2017. Elon Musk: We Need to Regulate AI Before it's Too Late. *The Hill*.

Erdelyi, J. Olivia, and Judy Goldsmith. 2018. Regulating Artificial Intelligence: Proposal for a Global Solution. AIES, 95–101.

Ganuza Juan Jose, and Fernando Gomez. 2005. Being Soft on Tort. Optimal Negligence Rule under Limited Liability. *Economics Working Papers 759*, Department of Economics and Business, Universitat Pompeu Fabra.

Gibbs, Samuel. 2017. Elon Musk: regulate AI to combat 'existential threat' before it's too late. *The Guardian*.

Herbig, A. Paul, and James E. Golden. 1994. Differences in Forecasting Behavior between Industrial Product Firms and Consumer Product Firms. *Journal of Business & Industrial Marketing* 1: 60–69.

Huberman, Gur, David Mayers, and Clifford W. Smith. 1983. Optimal Insurance Policy Indemnity Schedules. *Bell Journal of Economics* 14 (2): 415–426.

Keeton, R. William, and Evan Kwerel. 1984. Externalities in Automobile Insurance and the Underinsured Driver Problem. *Journal of Law and Economics* 27 (1): 149–179.

Kosinski, Michal, and Wang Yilun. 2018. Deep Neural Networks are more Accurate than Humans at Detecting Sexual Orientation from Facial Images. *Journal of Personality and Social Psychology* 114 (2): 246–257.

Kovac, Mitja. 2020. Autonomous AI and Uncontemplated Hazards: Towards an Optimal Regulatory Framework. *European Journal of Risk Regulation*.

Kraakman, H. Reimer. 2000. Vicarious and Corporate Civil Liability. In *Encyclopaedia of Law and Economics*, ed. Gerrit De Geest Gerrit, and Boudewijn Bouckaert, Volume II. Civil Law and Economics. Cheltenham: Edward Elgar.

Malott, Richard W. 1988. Rule-Governed Behavior and Behavioral Anthropology. *The Behavior Analyst* 11 (2): 181–203.

McGuire, Jean B. 2016. A Dialectical Analysis of Interorganizational Networks. *Journal of Management* 14 (1): 109–124.

Russell, Stuart. 2019. *Human Compatible*. London: Allen Lane.

Schäfer, Hans-Bernd, and Claus Ott. 2004. *The Economic Analysis of Civil Law*, 107–261. Cheltenham: Edward Elgar.

Shavell, Steven. 1986. The Judgement Proof Problem. *International Review of Law and Economics* 6: 45–58.

Turing, Alan. 1951. *Intelligent Machinery, a Heretical Theory*. Lecture given to the 51 Society, Manchester.

Wadhwa, V. 2014. Laws and Ethics Can't Keep Pace with Technology. *Massachusetts Institute of Technology: Technology Review* 15.

PART I

Conceptual Framework

CHAPTER 2

Economic Analysis of Law

Abstract This chapter offers a synthesis of the employed law and economics methodology and provides an overview of the concepts of rationality, risk-aversion, transaction cost phenomena, and investigates the nature of economic reasoning. It also offers a brief historical narrative of the employed methodology and investigates the relationship between the positive and normative analysis. Moreover, this chapter also provides a brief summary on the rational and irrational human decision-making process, maximization of utility and welfare on the notion of behavioural law and economics, and offers a general implication and evidences of boundedly rational and non-rational human behaviour.

Keywords Law and economics · Transaction cost · Wealth maximization · Rationality · Risk-aversion · Behavioural law and economics · Decision-making · Methodology

1 Introduction

This chapter introduces the basic methods and tools of the law and economics approach employed throughout this book. It focuses on the question, how does law and economics differ from other ways of thinking about artificial intelligence, social fabric, and legal institutions?

M. Kovač, *Judgement-Proof Robots and Artificial Intelligence*,
https://doi.org/10.1007/978-3-030-53644-2_2

After a decade of thorough comparative investigation almost every civilian lawyer, trained and educated on the European continent, sooner or later realizes that common law scholars have actually always been occupied with three questions seen also as central to the law and economics enterprise. Namely, the first question, that English scholars are concerned with, is what is the effect of given law and how will people behave in response to it? Second, what the law should be? Third, what can we expect the law to be and what explains the structure and the texture of the law that we observe? These questions are, as Cohen and Wright emphasizes, also the core subjects of law and economics movement (Cohen and Wright 2009). So, then, what is novel and groundbreaking in the law and economics?

The novelty of the law and economics research programs lies in its search of what good law is by analysing incentive, risk, and transaction costs effects of legal rules. It attempts to determine which legal have the most desirable effects and offers also useful advice on how to improve the technical formulation of the rules (De Geest 2001). The reason is that "lawmakers usually balance the advantages and disadvantages of alternative solutions, even though this balancing is often hidden behind the veil of fairness rhetoric" (De Geest and Kovac 2009). Law and economics seeks to describe these advantages and disadvantages in a more accurate, economically informed, way. As a result, as De Geest and Kovac (2009) suggest it may also "accurately describe what lawmakers do, and hence, more accurately describe the law."

Hence, throughout this book, the approach is interdisciplinary, focusing on legal and economic issues. Whereas an economic approach or as generally referred to as the "law and economics" is becoming increasingly common and influential in the study of substantive contract, tort, and competition law of the United States and some European countries, its application in the analysis of artificial intelligence evolved relatively recently and is positioned at the frontiers of progressive legal thought. This innovative scholarly paradigm, combining the analytical tools of adjoining and complementary social sciences in order to develop a critical approach to legal rules and institutions, conveys a distinctive comparative perspective on the theory, practice, and understanding of the law of different legal systems. The approach utilized in this book combines analytical methods and concepts used in the classic comparative law and economics and enriches them with the behavioural law and economics discussions. However, in order to provide an overview of applied methodology, the concepts and methods of both concepts will be briefly summarized and then combined in a unified conceptual framework.

2 On the Nature of Economic Reasoning

In order to fully appraise the scope and possible impact of the comparative law and economics approach and having in mind that this book is written primarily for general audience a short introduction into the nature of economic reasoning and "traditional" rational choice economics has to be offered. Namely, many judges, lawyers, and surprisingly even some students of business and management still think that economics is the study of economic depressions, deflation, inflation, underemployment, globalization, exploitation, austerity, quantitative easing, banking, elasticity, and other mysterious phenomena remote from the day-to-day concerns of the legal and economic system (Posner 2014). However, the domain of economics, as the queen of social sciences, is much broader and economics itself may be actually regarded as a science of human behaviour (Becker 1976). The traditional, orthodox economics is science of rational choice in a world in which resources are limited in relation to human needs and rests on the assumption that a man is a rational, wealth maximizing, self-interested, and risk-averse person (Becker 1976). Traditional economics hence assumes that a man rationally maximizes his ends in life (self-interest). This concept of "rational wealth-maximization" should not be confused with conscious calculation and economics is not a theory about consciousness (Posner 2014, 1979). Human behaviour is in this respect rational when it conforms to the model of rational choice (whatever the state of mind of that chooser is). This concept is objective rather than subjective and rationality means to traditional economist little more than a disposition to choose, consciously or unconsciously, an apt means to whatever ends the chooser happens to have (Posner 2014). Rationality is hence merely the ability and inclination to use instrumental reasoning to get on in life. Some economists also employ the term "bounded rationality" to describe the rationality of rational persons who face positive costs of acquiring, absorbing, processing, and of using the information (transaction costs) available to them to make their decisions (Simon 1976). The term "bounded rationality" was actually introduced by Herbert Simon in 1955 and refers to the cognitive limitations facing decision-makers in terms of acquiring and processing information (Simon

1955). In other words, it may be argued that almost all human decisions are actually "boundedly rational" since they are made in the world of imperfect information and positive transaction costs.

Moreover, the concept of self-interest should also not be confused with selfishness, since misery and the happiness of other people might be part of one's satisfactions. Evidently, economics also assumes that man is a rational utility maximizer in all areas of life, not just in his economic affairs (i.e. not only when they are engaged in buying and selling). This concept of man as a rational, wealth maximizing, self-interested individual person also implies that people respond to incentives in a generally predictable way (Hindmoor 2006). For example, if a person's surroundings change in such a way that she could increase her satisfaction by altering her behaviour, she will do so (Cooter and Ulen 2011). This rational choice concept that encompasses the traditional economic analysis has been in recent years challenged on several grounds beside the very superficial one that it does not describe how people think about or describe their decisions (Posner 2014; Hindmoor 2006). Of course, this conventional "rational" approach does not assume at all that persons have always perfect information and consequently also persons which do not have perfect information *ex ante* are still making, in the light of their imperfect information, *ex ante* rational decisions. If the *ex ante* costs of acquiring and processing more information exceed the expected benefits of having more information and in making a better decision, then decisions made under such circumstances are actually still rational ones, though they might *ex post* appear as completely irrational ones. Moreover, if one would in such circumstances strife for perfect *ex ante* information then this kind of behaviour would be actually an irrational one or at least inefficient one. Finally, one should also note, that economics as a science is concerned with explaining and predicting aggregates rather than behaviour of each individual person (Rodrik 2015).

3 Methodology and Concepts Used in the Economic Analysis of Law

As emphasized, the "law and economics" is one of the most ambitious and probably the most influential concepts that seek to explain judicial decision-making and to place it on an objective basis. It is regarded as the single most influential jurisprudential school in the United States

(Hatzis and Mercuro 2015; Posner 2014, 2001). Although a comprehensive examination of the field is beyond the scope of this book and can be found elsewhere (Cohen and Wright 2009; Polinsky and Shavell 2007; Shavell 2007; Katz 1998), the basic approach will be outlined. The central assumption of economics is that all people (except children and mentally disabled) are rational maximizers of their satisfactions in all of their activities. In other words, the rational choice approach is the basic methodological principle in this book, which besides maximizing behaviour and market equilibrium, also comprises the assumption of stable preferences (Georgakopoulus 2005). The notion of maximizing behaviour comprises the principle of wealth maximization, where the measure for parties' maximizing behaviour is their willingness to pay (Kerkmeester 1999). That is to say, if goods are in the hands of the persons who were willing and able to pay the highest amount, wealth is maximized (Posner 2011). Wealth maximization is also applied as the leading principle of analysis.

3.1 Wealth Maximization

One of the main fallacies is to equate business income to social wealth. Wealth maximization refers to a sum of all tangible goods and services, weighted by offer prices and asking prices (Posner 2014). The notion of wealth maximization is that the value of wealth in society should be maximized (Shavell 2007; Coleman 1988; Posner 1979). In this context wealth should be understood as the summation of all valued objects, both tangible and intangible, weighted by the prices they would command if they were to be traded in markets (Posner 2001). The transaction is wealth maximizing, where, providing that it has no third-party effects and is a product of free, unanimous choice, has made two people better off and no one worse off (Towfigh 2015). This is the so-called "Pareto–efficiency," where it is impossible to change it so as to make at least one person better off without making anyone worse off (Pareto 1909). Parties enter into transactions on the basis of rational self-interest where voluntary transactions tend to be mutually beneficial. Hence, the term "efficiency" used throughout this book denotes that allocation of resources whose value is maximized. As is common in modern economics, I will use the Kaldor–Hicks variant of the Pareto optimality criterion, according to which it is sufficient that the winners could, in theory, compensate the losers, even if this compensation is not effectively paid

(Kaldor 1939; Hick 1939). The assumption that those entering into exchanges are rationally self-interested is the basic assumption of law and economics.

3.2 Transaction Costs

The notion that the welfare of human society depends on the flow of goods and services, and this in turn depends on the productivity of the economic system can hardly be overstated (Coase 1988). This phenomenon was first discussed by Nobel prize winner Ronald Coase in his seminal articles (1937, 1960) and developed by other eminent authors (Williamson 1996). Namely, the productivity of the economic system depends on specialization which is only possible if there is an exchange of goods and services. Such an exchange, a voluntary transaction is beneficial to both parties, but transaction costs than reduce the value of an exchange and both contracting parties will want to minimize them. Transaction costs thus slow the movement of scarce resources to their most valuable uses and should be minimized in order to spur allocative efficiency. In other words, the amount of that exchanges which spur allocative efficiency depends, as Coase (Coase 1988) and North (1990) argue, also upon the costs of exchange—the lower they are the more specialization there will be and the greater the productivity of the system (Coase 1937, 1960). In a world of zero transaction costs, parties would always produce economically efficient results without the need for legal intervention. However, since transaction costs are imposed daily, intervention becomes necessary and the legal rules by reducing transaction costs imposed upon an exchange can improve (or worsen in case of increased transaction costs) allocative efficiency and thus maximize social welfare.

Transaction costs, in the original formulation by Coase (1937, 1988, 1994), are defined as "the cost of using the price mechanism" or "the cost of carrying out a transaction by means of an exchange on the open market." As Coase (1960) explains, "In order to carry out a market transaction it is necessary to discover who it is that one wishes to deal with, to inform people that one wishes to deal and on what terms, to conduct negotiations leading up to a bargain, to draw up the contract, to undertake the inspection needed to make sure that the terms of the contract are being observed, and so on." Coase actually sees transaction costs as a crucial factor in shaping the institutions, including law that determines the allocation of resources (Polinsky and Shavell 2007). Any allocation of resources to more productive uses would be achieved immediately and we would be all in an ideal world of allocative efficiency (Demsetz 2002).

Arrow (1969), De Geest (1994), Williamson (1996), and Posner (2011), while closely resembling Coase's concept, insightfully define transaction costs as the costs of running the economic system of exchanges—costs of exchange. For example, when Robinson Crusoe was alone on the island, there were no transaction costs—as soon as Friday arrived, and they started working together, transaction costs appear. Here, one should note that transaction costs are not costs like the production costs or precaution costs (which Robinson would also have if one would want to have the optimal pollution on his island) but merely costs of economic exchanges. Coase's (1960) definition of transaction costs actually encompasses *ex ante* costs (before the exchange) associated with search, negotiation, and *ex post* costs (after exchange) of monitoring and enforcement.

3.3 Uncertainty and Risks

Economists established that one of the basic characteristics of economic actors is their attitude towards risks. Economists believe that most people are risk-averse most of the time, although a number of institutional responses (such as insurance contracts and corporations) may make people act as if they are risk-neutral in many situations (Posner 2014; Bell et al. 1988). Risk-averse people are willing to pay more than the expected value of a possible loss to eliminate the risk therein (Shavell 2007; Sunstein 2007; Shafir and LeBoeuf 2002). A person will be risk-averse if the marginal utility of money to him declines as his wealth increases (Kreps 1990). The widespread use of insurances witnesses the value of this argument, where risk-averse persons are prepared to pay insurance premiums for not having to suffer the losses when risks occur (Shavell 1987). In contrast, a risk-loving person places a value on risk lower than the expected value of the losses, whereas a risk-neutral person places a value on risk equal to the expected value of the losses (Krep 1990; Shavell 1987).

Economic theory suggests that whenever one person can bear the risk at lower costs than another, efficiency requires assigning the risk upon such a superior risk bearer (Calabresi 1972; Brown 1973; Arrow 1963; Posner and Rosenfield 1977). In such an instance there is an opportunity for mutually beneficial exchange, where risk-averse persons are willing to pay risk-neutral persons to bear such risks. In cases where transaction costs preclude parties from making such an arrangement, efficiency offers a hypothetical bargain approach of the most efficient risk bearer (Posner and Rosenfield 1977). Such a bearer is the party to an exchange who is best able to minimize the losses. It should be noted that almost any contract shifts risks, since contracts by their nature commit the parties to a future course of action, where the future is far from certain.

4 Comparative Law and Economics

Classic functional micro-comparative law method, employed in comparative legal scholarship (Markesinis 1997; Zweigert and Kötz 1998) though highly insightful, might need additional analytical tools for establishing which of the compared legal regimes is better, since the specific function itself cannot serve as benchmark, and since as comparatists point out, once the similarity has been established the same function cannot determine superiority, making a comprehensive evaluation almost impossibly complex (Michaels 2008). Moreover, the evaluation criteria should be different from the criteria of comparability. Yet the evaluation criteria is defined as a "practical judgment" or "policy decision" under the conditions of partial uncertainty (Michaels 2008). Obviously, such evaluation criteria might be open to subjective interpretation. Instead, I argue, law and economics may offer an alternative conceptual framework complementing, enriching classic functional micro-comparison. Such a method is known in literature as comparative law and economics (Mattei 1997), which treats the legal and institutional backgrounds as dynamic variables and attempts to build models which reflect the ever-changing layered complexity of the real world of law.

Employed comparative law and economics employs analytical tools to evaluate and explain analogies and differences among alternative legal patterns. This examination offers instructive insight into which of the compared legal systems is more or less efficient, provides economic explanations for judicial decisions and statutory provisions and enables measurement of the actual difference or analogy of the compared systems. Hence, by supplementing traditional comparative law methodology with an economic analysis of law, this book offers additional instructive insights and supplements otherwise inconclusive evaluation.

Moreover, in order to make the economic analysis accessible to the audience not acquainted with sophisticated mathematical reasoning the employed law and economics toolkit follows the classical comparative law and economics approach (Bergh van den 2018). As advocated by Professor Van den Bergh (2018), one of the founding fathers of law and economics movement in Europe, the essence of this approach is to "bridge the gap between economic theory, empirical studies and policy proposals for an improved legal system." This classical comparative law and economics approach serve as a "bridge between facts and normative conclusions" (Bergh van den 2018).

4.1 Positive and Normative Economic Analysis

One of the central questions of economics is the question of choice under conditions of scarcity and the related attempts of individuals to maximize their desired ends by doing the best they can with the limited resources at their disposal (formation of preferences). In analysing the question of choice neoclassical economics employs two conceptually different kinds of analysis (Trebilcock 1993). The first is the so-called positive analysis and the second is normative analysis. This distinction between positive and normative analysis is almost 200 years old, going back to the writings of John Stuart Mill. This familiar distinction, as Blaug (1980) argues in economics became entangled with a distinction among philosophical positivists between "is" and "ought," between facts and values, between supposedly objective, declarative statements about the world and prescriptive evaluations of states of the world.

As Friedman says, the task of positive analysis is "to provide a system of generalizations that can be used to make correct predictions about consequences of any change in circumstances" and it deals with "what is," not with "what ought to be" (Friedman 1953).

However, in the 1990s, a new generation of literature developed on the intersection of law, economics, and public choice theory studying the origins and formative mechanisms of legal rules (Klick and Parisi 2015). Klick and Parisi (2015) suggest the employment of the functional law and economics approach which avoids paternalism and methodological imperialism by formulating value-neutral principles of collective choice. Such functional law and economics approach represents a mode of analysis that "bridges both the positive and normative schools of thought in law and economics" (Klick and Parisi 2015).

The comparative law and economic analysis in this book is equally positive and normative. It is positive (what the law is) since it tends to ask the questions of what kind of predictions can we make as to the probable economics impacts if certain rule (such as allocating a special legal personality to the autonomous artificial intelligence) and how individuals and institutions might respond to the particular incentives or disincentives created by such rules or policies. It is also normative (what the law ought to be) since it provides suggestion for an improved regulatory regime, which promotes wealth maximization and "increase the size of the pie." (Coleman 1982; Posner 1979). Hence, it provides rules which should govern in order to maximize social welfare.

5 Behavioural Law and Economics

In the last two decades, social scientists and law and economics scholars have learned a great deal about how people actually make their decisions. The newly developed field of economics, which was inspired by a triggering difference between the predicted and actual behaviour of rational, self-interested, risk-averse person, the behavioural economics, borrowing from psychology and sociology to explain decisions inconsistent with traditional economics, has revolutionized the way economists (and to lesser extent also lawyers) view the world (Akerlof 2002; Teck et al. 2006; Wilkinson 2008; Diamond and Vartiainen 2007). Moreover, policymakers, regulators, judges, and competition authorities are increasingly looking to the lessons from behavioural economics to help them determine whether markets are working in the interest of consumers.

The observed behavioural inconsistencies and apparent shortcomings of the conventional economic approach have induced some scholars to investigate the underlying motivation behind the behaviour of people in order to improve previously discussed theories and make more accurate predictions. Simon's pioneering work and introduction of "bounded rationality" (Simon 1955) has been followed by several significant contributions (Markowitz 1952; Allais 1953; Schelling 1960; Ellsberg 1961) and at the end of 1970 the field of behavioural economics was established. In 1979 Kahneman and Tversky (1979) published their groundbreaking article on prospect theory in which they introduced fundamental concepts in relation to reference points, loss aversion, utility measurement, and subjective probability judgements. This seminal work has been followed by Thaler's contribution on a positive theory of consumer choice where the concept of mental accounting has been introduced (Thaler 1980).

Moreover, this resurgence of psychology in economics has also inspired some legal scholars to employ additional scholarship in both cognitive psychology and behavioural economics, which suggests that human behaviour often deviates from rational choice in systematic and predictable ways, to explain legal phenomena and to argue for legal reforms (Langevoort 1998). This novel approach (methodology) is now known as the behavioural law and economics (Wilkinson 2008; Sunstein 2000).

Behavioural law and economics argues that persons display bounded rationality and that (a) suffer from certain biases, such as over-optimism and self-serving conceptions of fairness, (b) follow heuristics, such as availability, that lead to mistakes; (c) display incomplete self-control that induces persons to make decisions that are in the conflict with their long-term interest; and (d) they behave in accordance with prospect theory rather than expected utility theory (Jolls et al. 2000). Moreover, people might have bounded willpower and they might be tempted and myopic (Jolls et al. 2000). Furthermore, people might be concerned by the well-being of the others and this concern and their self-conception can lead them in the direction of cooperation at the expense of their material self-interest (Jolls 2007; Jolls et al. 2000).

Jolls et al. (2000) also suggest that behavioural insights shall be employed in order to better explain both the effects and the content of the law. Such insights should be employed to help the lawmaker to achieve specified ends, such as deterring socially undesirable behaviour. Yet, one might also argue that all of the discussed behavioural insights and observed inconsistencies could be also neatly explained from the conventional law and economics perspective. Observed patterns, behavioural biases might actually be a result of the completely rational *ex ante* decision-making which has been made in a world of positive transaction costs and asymmetric information. In other words, the employed methodological framework, assumptions, and definitions might determine also the lawyers' normative and positive analysis, conclusions, and suggestions.

5.1 General Implications and Evidences of Non-Rational Behaviour

As discussed previously conventional law and economics assumes that people exhibit rational behaviour: that people are risk-averse, self-interested utility maximizers with stable preferences and the capacity to optimally accumulate and assess information. However, a large body of social science literature demonstrates that these assumptions are not always accurate and that deviations from rational behaviour are often semantic (Vandenberghe 2011). Based on this evidence Jolls et al. (2000) claim that people exhibit bounded rationality, bounded self-interest, and bounded willpower. Behaviourists offer ample evidence that cognitive limitations force actors to employ relatively simple decision-making strategies which may cause actors to fail to maximize their utility (Simon 1972; Morwitz et al. 1998; Fischhoff and Beyth 1975; Gabaix and Laibson 2006; Jolls 2007; Luth 2010; Stucke 2012). What follows is a brief synthesis of these general implications, heuristic and biases that are of the particular relevance to the law.

Firstly, persons are averse to extremes which gives rise to compromise effects. For example, as Sunstein (2000) argues, almost everyone of us has had the experience of switching to the second most expensive dish on the food menu and of doing so partly because of the presence of the most expensive dish. In other words, persons might have great difficulties judging probabilities, making predictions, and coping with uncertainties. Availability heuristics introduced by Kahneman and Tversky (1974) is another source of our errors in relation to risk perception, since persons tend to judge the probability of a future event based on the ease with which instances can be brought to mind. Hence, people might weight disproportionally salient, memorable, or vivid evidence, despite the fact that they might have better, scientific sources of information. Slovic and Lichtenstein (1971) identified anchoring and adjustment as another source of human errors, arguing that there is a tendency to make probability judgements on the basis of an initial value-anchor, to resist altering such a probability estimate, even when pertinent new information comes to light. People also suffer from the overconfidence, self-serving bias, and over-optimism. Moreover, people also tend to overestimate the occurrence of low probability risks and underestimate the occurrence of high-probability risks. For example, we all experienced a prevailing fear of flying (and having a crash) while the aeroplane is taking off from the airport although the probability of an accident is a minor one, whereas we never think about having a car accident while driving our cars although the probability of such an event is a significant one. Simply, we think that such risks are less likely for materialize to ourselves than for others. This notion in behavioural economics is described as the "optimistic bias" (Tversky and Kahneman 1974). Humans actually tend to be optimistic but this over-optimism can lead us to make fatal mistakes. Namely, if people tend to believe that they are relatively free from risks, they may lack accurate information even if they know statistical facts and hence this optimistic bias might be an argument for the paternalism in lawmaking.

Secondly, literature offers ample evidence of hindsight biases where people often think in hindsight, that things that happened were inevitable, or nearly so (Sunstein 2000). People also tend to like the *status quo*, and they demand a great deal to justify departures from it (Sunstein 2000). People actually evaluate situations largely in accordance with their relation to a certain reference point and the departed gains or losses from that reference point are prevailing in their decision to change the *status quo* position.

Thirdly, the identified endowment effect introduced by Thaler (1980) stands for the principle that people tend to value goods more when they own them than when they do not. A consequence of such an endowment effect is, according to Thaler (1980), the "offer-asking gap," which is the empirically observed phenomenon that people will often demand a higher price to sell a good that they already possess than they would pay for the same good if they did not possess it at present. Kahneman and Tversky (1974) explain all of this observed patterns and inconsistencies as a result of "loss aversion" where losses from a reference point are valued more highly than equivalent gains. Hence, making one option the status quo or endowing a person with a good seems to establish a reference point from which people depart from only very reluctantly, or if they are paid a large sum (Tversky and Kahneman 1974; Thaler and Sunstein 2008). Thaler (1980) explains this endowment effect as a simple underweighting of opportunity costs. Hence, if out of pockets losses are viewed by persons as losses and opportunity costs are viewed as foregone gains, the former will be more heavily weighted and people's decision-making will reflect that weighting. Thus, as Thaler (1980) advances, a person would be willing to pay more in opportunity costs to keep a good that he already possesses than he would be willing to spend in received income (out-of-pocket money) to acquire the good.

The previously discussed endowment effect, status quo bias and default preference might, as argued by Vandenberghe (2011), undermine the central premise of conventional law and economics where fully informed individuals allowed to exercise free choice will maximize their own utility, and thus social welfare, when transaction costs are low. Under such assumptions, legal systems might not maximize social welfare by simply following the standard assumptions of economics and allow markets to operate whenever possible (Vandenberghe 2011). However, one should note that the assumption of zero or at least very low transaction costs is never satisfied and that the transaction costs are always positive, very often even prohibitive.

To sum up, the behavioural law and economics argues that people, while making their daily decisions, display (a) bounded rationality; (b) they suffer from certain biases, such as over-optimism and self-serving conceptions of fairness; (c) they follow heuristics, such as availability, which leads to mistakes; and (d) they behave in accordance with prospect theory rather than expected utility theory (Jolls et al. 2000). Moreover, according to Jolls et al. (2000) people also have bounded willpower, are boundedly self-interested, they can be tempted and can be even myopic. They insightfully also argue that people are on average concerned about the well-being of others, even strangers in some circumstances and this self-conception might lead them in the direction of cooperation at the expense of their material, narrowly defined, rational self-interest (Thaler and Sunstein 2008; Jolls 2007; Jolls et al. 2000).

6 Obstacles to an Economic Approach

There are different reasons why lawyers, officials, and judges may be hesitant to adopt a full-fledged economic approach to contract or tort law. Van den Bergh (2016) offers two main reasons: (a) they may subject to the cognitive bias that an economic approach boils down to an adoption of Chicago views, which are seen as ultraliberal and politically biased in favour of the interests of large industry groups and (b) they may have great difficulties in accepting the results of economic analysis that are counter-intuitive and contradict common expectations and ideas.

In European discussions about regulatory policy, the term Chicago has a negative connotation and shooting at Chicago remains a popular sport. By contrast, in the United States, Chicago economics has established itself as a main component of industrial organization theory (Williamson 1981). The Harvard paradigm and the Chicago paradigm are not incompatible as organizing principles and may, therefore, be used as complementary rather than as mutually exclusive. The Harvard School for example supported market interventionism and argued that a concentrated market structure has a negative impact on the conduct of firms in the market and on ultimate market performance. Whereas the Chicago

School reacted to this interventionism by postulating the rival paradigm of economic efficiency (Bergh van den 2016). Firms grow big because they are more efficient than their rivals and persistent market concentration is the result of the need to achieve minimum efficient scale and not of collusion.

7 Conclusions

Discussed law and economics approach dominates the intellectual discussion of nearly every doctrinal area of law in the United States and its presence its again gaining relevance across the European continent. After several decades of groundbreaking work and despite its controversy the law and economics is now securely niched within legal (and economic) academy. It has proved to be a very powerful tool to structure a policy debate and to analyse the potential effectiveness and/or efficiency of policy choices. One of its founding fathers, Justice Richard Posner, even argues that "law and economics promotes certain scholarly virtues that are sorely needed in legal scholarship and that it has a broad scope of relatively uncontroversial application" (Posner 2015).

As showed, by adopting an *ex ante* approach, law and economics provides information about the real-life effects of legislation, regulatory intervention, and case law that remain hidden in an *ex post* perspective. Law and economics also provides a framework to structure the policy discussion and enables substantive understanding of the core of the problem and boost recognition of false arguments. Discussed methodology, narrative of positive and normative analysis and sketched behavioural insights will be in the rest of this book employed as a conceptual framework facilitating our investigation of autonomous artificial intelligence and its potential hazards.

Bibliography

Akerlof, Geoffrey. 2002. Behavioral Macroeconomics and Macroeconomic Behaviour. *American Economics Review* 92 (1): 411–433.

Allais, Maurice. 1953. Fondements d'une Theorie Positive des Choix Comportant un Risque et Critique des Postulats et Axiomes de L'Ecole Americaine. *Econometrica* 21 (4): 503–546.

Arrow, J. Kenneth. 1963. Uncertainty and the Welfare Economics of Medical Care. *American Economic Review* 53: 941–973.

Becker, S. Garry. 1976. *The Economic Approach to Human Behaviour*. Chicago: University of Chicago Press.

Bell, E. David, Howard Raiffa, and Amos Tversky (eds.). 1988. *Decision Making: Descriptive, Normative and Prescriptive Interactions*. New York: Cambridge University Press.

Bergh van den, Roger. 2016. The More Economic Approach in European Competition Law: Is More Too Much or Not Enough? In *Economic Evidence in EU Competition Law*, ed. Mitja Kovac and Ann-Sophie Vandenberghe, 13–44. Intersentia.

Bergh van den, Roger. 2018. *The Roundabouts of European Law and Economics*. Den Haag: Eleven International Publishing.

Blaug, Mark. 1980. *Methodology of Economics: Or, How Economists Explain*. Cambridge: Cambriidge University Press.

Brown, J.P. 1973. Towards an Economic Theory of Liability. *Journal of Legal Studies* 2: 323–349.

Calabresi, Guido. 1972. *The Costs of Accidents: A Legal and Economic Analysis*. New Haven: Yale University Press.

Coase, H. Ronald. 1937. The Nature of the Firm. *Econometrica* 4: 394.

Coase, H. Ronald. 1960. The Problem of Social Cost. *Journal of Law and Economics* 1 (3): 1–44.

Coase, H. Ronald. 1988. *The Firm, the Market and the Law*. Chicago: University of Chicago Press.

Coase, H. Ronald. 1994. *Essays on Economics and Economists*. Chicago: University of Chicago Press.

Cohen, Lloyd R., and Joshua D. Wright. 2009. Introduction. In *Pioneers of Law and Economics*, ed. Lloyd R. Cohen, and Joshua D. Wright, vii–viii. Cheltenham: Edward Elgar.

Coleman, Jules. 1982. The Normative Basis of Economic Analysis: A Critical Review of Richard Posner's The Economics of Justice. *Stamford Law Review* 34: 1105–1131.

Coleman, Jules. 1988. *Markets, Morals and the Law*. Cambridge: Cambridge University Press.

Cooter, Robert, and Thomas Ulen. 2011. *Law and Economics*, 6th ed. New Jersey: Prentice Hall.

De Geest, Gerrit. 1994. *Economische Analyse van het Contracten- en Quasi-Contractenrecht*. Antwerpen: Maklu.

De Geest, Gerrit. 2001. Comparative Law and Economics and the Design of Optimal Doctrines. In *Law and Economics in Civil Law Countries*, ed. Bruno Deffains, and Tom Kirat, 107–124. New York: JAI Elsevier.

De Geest, Gerrit, and Mitja Kovac. 2009. The Formation of Contracts in the Draft Common Frame of Reference. *European Review of Private Law* 17 (2): 113–132.

Demsetz, Harold. 2002. Toward a Theory of Property Rights II: The Competition between Private and Collective Ownership. *The Journal of Legal Studies* 31 (2): 653–672.

Diamond, Peter, and Hannu Vartiainen. 2007. *Behavioral Economics and its Applications*. New Jersey: Princeton University Press.

Eldar, Shafir, and Robin A. LeBoeuf. 2002. Rationality. *Annual Review of Psychology* 53: 491.

Ellsberg, Daniel. 1961. Risk, Ambiguity and the Savage Axiom. *Quarterly Journal of Economics* 75 (4): 643–669.

Fischhoff, B., and R. Beyth. 1975. 'I Knew it Would Happen': Remembered Probabilities of Once-Future Things. *Organizational Behaviour and Human Performance* 13 (1): 1–16.

Friedman, Milton. 1953. *Essays in Positive Economics*. Chicago: University of Chicago Press.

Gabaix, X., and D. Laibson. 2006. Shrouded Attributes, Consumer Myopia and Information Suppression in Competitive Markets. *121 Quarterly Journal of Economics* 2: 505–540.

Georgakopoulus, L. Nicholas. 2005. *Principles and Methods of Law and Economics: Basic Tools for Normative Reasoning*. Cambridge: Cambridge University Press.

Hatzis, Aristides N., and Nicholas Mercuro (eds.). 2015. *Law and Economics: Philosophical Issues and Fundamental Questions*. New York: Routledge.

Hicks, R. John. 1939. The Foundations of Welfare Economics. *Economic Journal* 49 (2): 696.

Hindmoor, Andrew. 2006. *Rational Choice*. Basingstoke: Palgrave MacMillan.

Jolls, Christine. 2007. Behavioral law and economics. In *Behavioral Economics and its Applications*, ed. Peter Diamond and Hannu Vartiainen, 115 et seq. Princeton University Press.

Jolls, Christine, R. Cass Sunstein, and Richard H. Thaler. 2000. A Behavioral Approach to Law and Economics. In Behavioral Law and Economics, ed. Sunstein, R. Cass, 13–58. Cambridge University Press.

Kahneman, Daniel and Amos Tversky. 1979. Prospect Theory: An Analysis of Decisions under Risk. 47 *Econometrica* 47: 263.

Kaldor, Nicholas. 1939. Welfare Propositions of Economics and Interpersonal Comparisons of Utility. *Economic Journal* 49 (2): 549.

Katz, W. Avery (ed.). 1998. *Foundations of the Economic Approach to Law*. New York: Oxford University Press.

Kerkmeester, Heico. 1999. Methodology: General. In *Encyclopedia of Law and Economics*, ed. Boudewijn Bouckaert and Gerrit De Geest. Cheltenham: Edward Elgar.

Klick, Jonathan, and Francesco Parisi. 2015. Functional Law and Economics. In *Law and Economics: Philosophical Issues and Fundamental Questions*, ed. Aristides N. Hatzis and Nicholas Mercuro, 1–16. New York: Routledge.

Kreps, M. David. 1990. *A Course in Microeconomic Theory*. New Jersey: Princeton University Press.

Langevoort, C. Douglas. 1998. Behavioral Theories of Judgment and Decision Making in Legal Scholarship: A Literature Review. *Vanderbilt Law Review* 51 (6 November 1998): 1499–1540.

Luth, A. Hanneke. 2010. *Behavioural Economics in Consumer Policy: The Economic Analysis of Standard Terms in Consumer Contracts Revisited*. Cambridge: Intersentia.

Markesinis, S. Basil. 1997. *Foreign Law and Comparative Methodology: A Subject and a Thesis*. London: Hart Publishing.

Markowitz, Harry. 1952. The Utility of Wealth. *Journal of Political Economy* 60 (2).

Mattei, Ugo. 1997. *Comparative Law and Economics*. Ann Arbor: The University of Michigan Press.

Michaels, Ralf. 2008. The Functional Method of Comparative Law. In *The Oxford Handbook of Comparative Law*, ed. Mathias Reimann and Reinhardt Zimmermann, 340–344. Oxford: Oxford University Press.

Morwitz, V.G., E.A. Greenleaf, and E.J. Johnson. 1998. Divide and Prosper: Consumers' Reactions to Partitioned Prices. *Journal of Marketing Research* 35 (1): 453–463.

Morwitz, V., E. Greenleaf, E. Shaelev, and E.J. Johnson. 2009. *The Price does not Include Additional Taxes, Fees and Surcharges: A Review of Research on Partitioned Pricing*.

North, C. Douglas. 1990. *Institutions, Institutional Change and Economic Performance*. New York: Cambridge University Press.

Pareto, Vilfredo. 1909. *Manuel d'Économie Politique*. Paris: V. Giard & E. Briére.

Polinsky, Mitchell A., and Steven Shavell (eds.). 2007. *The Handbook of Law and Economics*, Vol. I, Vol. II. Amsterdam: North-Holland.

Posner, A. Richard. 1979. Utilitarianism, Economics, and Legal Theory. *Journal of Legal Studies* 8: 103.

Posner, A. Richard. 2001. *Frontiers of Legal Theory*. Cambridge: Harvard University Press.

Posner, A. Richard. 2011. *Economic Analysis of Law*, 7th ed. New York: Aspen Publishers.

Posner, A. Richard. 2014. *Economic Analysis of Law*, 8th ed. New York: Aspen Publishers.

Posner, A. Richard. 2015. Norms and Values in the Study of Law. In *Law and Economics: Philosophical Issues and Fundamental Questions*, ed. Aristides N. Hatzis and Nicholas Mercuro, 1–16. New York: Routledge.

Posner, A. Richard, and A. Rosenfield. 1977. Impossibility and Related Doctrines in Contract Law: An Economic Analysis. *Journal of Legal Studies* 88.

Rodrik, Dani. 2015. *Economics Rules: The Rights and Wrongs of the Dismal Science*. New York: Norton.

Schelling, C. Thomas. 1960. *Strategy of Conflict*. Cambridge: Harvard University Pres.

Shavell, Steven. 1987. *Economic Analysis of Accident Law*. Cambridge: Harvard University Press.

Shavell, Steven. 2007. *Foundations of Economic Analysis of Law*. Cambridge: Harvard University Press.

Simon, A. Herbert. 1955. A Behavioral Model of Rational Choice. *Quarterly Journal of Economics* 69 (1): 99–118.

Simon, A. Herbert. 1972. Theories of Bounded Rationality. In "Decision and Organisation," North-Holland, ed. McGuire, C.B., and Ray Racher, North-Holland, 161–176.

Simon, A. Herbert. 1976. From Substantive to Procedural Rationality. In *25 Years of Economic Theory*, ed. T.J. Kastelei, S.K. Kuipers, W.A. Nijenhuis, and G.R. Wagenaar. Boston: Springer.

Slovic, P., and S. Lictensteln. 1971. Comparison of Bayesian and Regression Approaches to the Study of Information Processing in Judgment, 6 Organ. *Organizational Behavior and Human Performance* 4: 649–744.

Stucke, Maurice. 2012. Hearing on Competition and Behavioral Economics. Directorate for Financial and Enterprise Affairs Competition Committee, DAF/COMP/WD(2012)12.

Sunstein, R. Cass. 2000. *Behavioral Law and Economics*. Cambridge: Cambridge University Press.

Sunstein, R. Cass. 2007. Willingness to Pay Versus Welfare. *Harvard Law and Policy Review* 1 (2): 303–330.

Teck H. Ho, Noah Lim, and Colin F. Camerer. 2006. How "Psychological" Should Economic and Marketing Models Be? *Journal of Marketing Research* 43 (3): 341–344.

Thaler, Richard. 1980. Toward a Positive Theory of Consumer Choice. *Journal of Economic Behavior and Organization* 1 (l): 39–60.

Thaler, H. Richard, and Cass R. Sunstein. 2008. *Nudge. Improving Decisions about Health, Wealth and Happiness*. New Haven: Yale University Press.

Towfigh, V. Emanuel. 2015. The Economic Paradigm. In *Economic Methods for Lawyers*, ed. Emanuel V. Towfigh and Niels Petersen, 18–32. Cheltenham: Edward Elgar.

Trebilcock, J. Michael. 1993. *The Limits of Freedom of Contract*. Cambridge: Harvard University Press.

Tversky, Amon, and Daniel Kahneman. 1974. Judgment under Uncertainty: Heuristics and Biases. *Science* 185 (4157): 1124–1131.

Vandenberghe, Ann-Sophie. 2011. Behavioral Approaches to Contract Law. In *Contract Law and Economics, Vol.6, Encyclopedia of Law and Economics*, 2nd ed., ed. Gerrit De Geest. Edward Elgar.

Wilkinson, Nick. 2008. *An Introduction to Behavioral Economics*. Palgrave Macmillan.

Williamson, E. Oliver. 1981. The Economics of Organization: The Transaction Cost Approach. *American Journal of Sociology* 87 (3): 548–577.

Williamson, E. Oliver. 1996. *The Mechanisms of Governance*. New York: Oxford University Press.

Zweigert, Konrad, and Hein Kötz. 1998. *Introduction to Comparative Law*, 3rd ed. Oxford: Clarendon Press.

CHAPTER 3

The Case for Regulatory Intervention and Its Limits

Abstract This chapter addresses the issue of the balance between the state and the market. It examines the right scope and extent of regulatory intervention and discusses the question of whether a lawmaker should at all intervene into economy. Moreover, this chapter presents the conceptual foundations of the regulatory intervention. Furthermore, it provides a synthesis of the economic literature on why governments regulate and evaluates the advantages and disadvantages of the different forms of regulation, by involving an analysis of how firms respond to various kinds of incentives and controls offered by the government.

Keywords Perfect competition · Market failures · Negative externalities information asymmetries · Nature and scope of regulation

1 Introduction

In the previous chapter, we examined the methodological and conceptual framework employed throughout this book. In this chapter, we explore a crucial debate in law and economics and also in other social sciences concerning the balance between the state and the market. Which activities should be left to markets and which others should be the purview of the state? Classic law and economics textbooks suggest that such intervention is warranted only under clearly delineated circumstances.

M. Kovač, *Judgement-Proof Robots and Artificial Intelligence*,
https://doi.org/10.1007/978-3-030-53644-2_3

Among others, these include also the presence of "negative externalities," which materialize when actions by individual actors have major negative consequences for others that are not mediated via markets, paving the way for excessive level of some activities (Acemoglu and Robinson 2019). Economically speaking the potential hazards and damages caused by the uncontemplated activity of autonomous AI are a classic example of negative externalities and asymmetric information problem. Namely, the problem of positive transaction costs and asymmetric information results in the so-called market failures (Akerloff 1970) which cause suboptimal (inefficient) amount of economic activity and inefficient allocation of resources. Collective action problem, agency problem, tragedy of commons, and game theoretical prisoner's dilemma phenomena are the notorious embodiment of positive transaction costs and asymmetric information problems that generate negative externalities. The materialization of these negative externalities accompanied by the "private law failure" prima facie warrants the employment of the regulatory intervention in the public interest (Ogus 2004). In other words, allocative efficiency and optimal human behaviour will result only if decision-making process achieves 100% internalization of all external costs and benefits.

However, it has to be emphasized that the mere existence of market failures per se is not an adequate ground for the regulatory intervention. Such a regulatory intervention should take place if and only if the costs of such an intervention do not exceed the benefits of such an intervention. Namely, efficiency gains of such an intervention may be outweighed by market distortions, increased transaction cost, and other misallocations in other sectors of the economy fueled by such a regulatory intervention (Ogus 2004).

Moreover, the notorious "tragedy of commons" (Hardin 1968; Gordon 1954) concept suggests that individuals and/or firms might not see themselves as responsible for common resources such as public safety and might eventually destroy such common resource.

These problems can be, as it will be shown, remedied in several different ways and the law offers a plethora of different legal instruments including rules of civil liability, command and control public regulations, market-based instruments, "suasive" and voluntary instruments, and smart regulatory mixes.

2 A Nirvana World: Perfect Competition

The basic model of a market used in economics is that of perfect competition. Perfect competition and markets evolve towards a general equilibrium which is also a Pareto optimum. Recall from our previous discussion that in Pareto optimum no change in the allocation of resources anywhere could improve the lot of one or more participants without making someone worse off. MacKaay (2015) suggests that the Samuelson's demonstration of this result is one of the most remarkable successes of neoclassical economics in the first half of the twentieth century. The Adam Smith's (1776) invisible hand will push towards efficiency and markets left to themselves serve the public interest (MacKaay 2015).

The baseline model of a market used in law and economics is that of perfect competition, implying that no single agent in the market can influence the price (Morell 2015). In perfect competition "only agent's powerless but self-interested actions jointly generate the price" (Morell 2015). No single actor can influence the price and all agents are "price takers." In such a situation the price will be equal to the marginal willingness to pay and any supplier will adapt his output so that the last unit he supplied will just yield a revenue equal to the cost of producing that unit (Pindyck and Rubinfeld 2018). Resulted allocation of any resources generated by a perfectly competitive market is Pareto- and also Kaldor–Hicks-efficient (Pindyck and Rubinfeld 2018). Nobody can be made better off without making anybody worse off and any market equilibrium under perfect competition is Pareto-efficient (Morell 2015). Literature shows that in theory general equilibrium is possible where each market of the economy is in competitive equilibrium, and this constitutes equilibrium among all markets (Arrow and Debreu 1954; Varian 2010; Nicholson and Snyder 2008).

Saying all that, one may indeed wonder whether under such conditions a legal intervention in a market economy is at all justified? Do we really need legal intervention in a perfect market? The answer is a shocking one. Namely, even if markets function perfectly one would still need law to define what can be traded on markets. In other words, in the absence of property law and contract law (and related enforcement) there would be no market to study at all (or they will exist in a very rudimentary form—at arm's length). As Adam Smith (1776), the founding father of economics, observed trade and commerce can seldom flourish in the absence of the system of property rights and enforcement of contracts. In the absence of law there would be no markets and, for economists, nothing to study. Many markets do not exist simply because property rights are not defined or not enforceable (Morell 2015). In reality, as Morell (2015) states, "which markets exist and how they operate is shaped by legal practitioners defining property rights in their daily businesses."

However, such perfect markets, a kind of a "Nirvana world," in order to materialize and function perfectly (generating allocative efficiency and Pareto perfect world) require the fulfilment of several essential conditions, which are, to be precise, in real world solemnly met. Namely, "Nirvana world" needs fulfilment of following conditions: zero transaction cost; perfect information; competition in all markets; all goods are appropriated and can be exchanged in the market and its corollary, all production costs are imputed to the producers rather than imposed on third persons (zero externalities); and all market participants are fully informed regarding the choices open to them (Smith 1776; Samuelson 1947; Coase 1937; Coase 1960; Arrow and Debreu 1954; Akerloff 1970; Smith Barret 1974). Yet, as all of us can attest, there is no such thing as perfection and there is no such thing as a free lunch. Reality and its mysterious paths are actually witnessing a myriad of market imperfections that costs us dearly. In the following three sections we turn our attention to this omnipresent market imperfections phenomena.

3 Market Failures

Day-to-day markets are characterized by numerous, sometimes even systematic imperfections and is actually governed by extreme information asymmetries and non-trivial transaction cost problems. The conditions for the perfect markets to materialize are not fully satisfied in practice and consequently the allocation of goods by free markets is not efficient. Where they are not, there are said to be "market imperfections" or even "market failures" (Smith Barrett 1974). Classic law and economics textbooks as the most serious materializations of such imperfections list the following: (a) monopoly and other forms of distortions of competition; (b) collective public goods; (c) negative externalities; (d) incomplete or asymmetric information for some participants to a transaction; and (e) all other forms of transaction costs (Cooter and Ulen 2016; MacKaay 2015; Leiztel 2015; Posner 2014; Wittman 2006). However, it must be emphasized that supposed market failures are not in themselves sufficient ground for government correction (see below sub-chapter 3). This section briefly discusses two—information asymmetries and negative externalities—of these market failures instrumental for our discussion of judgement-proof autonomous artificial intelligence and optimal regulatory framework. In other words, literature suggests that supposed market failures are not in themselves sufficient ground for government correction.

3.1 Information Asymmetries

Almost every problem, every wrongful decision to act or not to act, every underestimation of potential hazards, risks, and damages is due to the notorious asymmetric information problem. Information is the essential ingredient of choice, and choice among scarce resources is also the central question of economics (Hirschleifer and Riley 1995; Schwartz and Scott 2007). Lack of information impairs one's ability to make decisions of the fully rational kind postulated in economic discourse, thus they must be made in the presence of uncertainty (MacKaay 1982). This uncertainty causes parties to make decisions different from what they would have made under conditions of abundant information. Such decisions may then entail a loss or failure to obtain a gain that could have been avoided with better information (MacKaay 1982). Uncertainty is thus generally a source of disutility, and information is the antidote to it. Namely, in most instances efficiency will be enhanced by moves that improve the flow of information in society.

Hence, also almost all legal problems are, in some way or another, a direct consequence of an imperfect information problem. Shaping laws that give parties an incentive to act in a way that leaves everyone better off is a straightforward matter, as long as all the parties and those who craft and enforce legal rules possess enough information. Complication arises when the necessary information is not known, or is known, but not to all parties, or not to the court (Baird et al. 2003). This holds especially for the remote, ex ante uncontemplated risks and hazards. If we assume that all agents have an infinite amount of information regarding their prospective relationship, activity, and the state of the world, then the issue of suboptimal precaution or mitigation of damages never arises. Parties would then simply always know all the relevant (as irrelevant) valuable, material facts and, if needed, contracted for, take precautionary measures, *ex ante* regulate potential market failures and deter moral hazard and opportunism. However, reality is far from that and the asymmetry of information crucially influences the market outcome.

In such circumstances, some of the information asymmetries might be corrected by the mechanism of voluntary exchange (Grossman 1981; Milgrom 1981), for example, by the seller's willingness to provide warranty to guarantee the quality of product (Grossman 1981; Milgrom 1981; Matthews and Postlewaite 1985; Cooter and Ulen 2016). Yet, distortions might be so significant that market mechanisms fail completely and the government intervention in the market becomes necessary, since it can ideally correct for the information asymmetries and induce more nearly optimal exchange (De Geest and Kovac 2009; Cooter and Ulen 2016).

Traditionally, legal doctrine has not been concerned with the definition of information, neither what constitutes information. The interest of legal scholars was mainly turned to the assessment of the legal nature of information—the discussion of whether information is a thing or not, thus if it is a service or a product. The reason is that the definition or nature of information has little legal consequences. For example, several legal authors who did discuss the liability of information provider did not provide any definition (Delebecque 1991), or merely a tautological one (Palandt 2002). More recently, with the development of information law, legal scholars have attempted to give a more precise, though still very broad, definition of what constitutes information. Pinna (2003) defines information as knowledge concerning persons or facts, and the provision of information is only the communication of knowledge, lacking an expressed or implied proposal to act.

Conversely, economics of information (Stigler 1961; Akerloff 1970; Koopmans and Montias 1971; Spence 1973, 1974) has developed a much more precise classification of the term, recognizing its multiple meanings. The distinction is driven between information as knowledge and as news. Knowledge is an accumulated body of data or evidence about the world. It is thus a stock of magnitude. When the world denotes an increment to this stock of knowledge, one speaks about message or news (Hirschliefer and Riley 1995). Knowledge and news are also objective evidence about the world, whereas belief is the subjective correlate of knowledge. Further, economics distinguishes between news and message, between messages and message service, between intended and inadvertent and inaccurate and deceptive communication (Hirschleifer and Riley 1995; Theil 1967). More important for our discussion is the difference between public and private information, based on its scarcity. At one extreme information may be possessed by only one individual (private information) and at the other, it may be known to everyone (public information). Publication is the conversion of information from private to public status. However, this book employs information in its broad general sense. Here "information" consists of events (data, news, knowledge, etc.) that tend to change the probability distribution. It is a change in belief distributions, which is a process and not a condition that constitutes the essence of information (Hirschleifer 1995).

3.2 Negative Externalities

Negative externality arises when one person's decision affects someone else, but where there is lack of institutional mechanism to induce the decision-maker to fully account for the spillover effect of their action or inaction (Leitzel 2015; Viscusi 2007, 1992; Coase 1959, 1960; Pigou 1932). These negative externalities can then also lead to market failures and the reason is that the generator of the externality does not have to pay for harming others, and so exercises too little self-restrain (Cooter and Ulen 2016; Miller et al. 2017; Hirshleifer 1984). For example, road traffic and cars contributing to global warming by emitting CO_2 without making it subject to transaction, smokers disturb non-smokers, graphited streets or trains disturb travellers and passers-by, and Covid-19 infected persons by disobeying self- isolating measures spreading the pathogen further.

In other words, the private cost to the person who creates the negative externality is smaller than the social cost, which is the sum of that private cost and the cost incurred by third persons (Pigou 1932; MacKaay 2015; Cooter and Ulen 2016). Corresponding public policies are then one of the most effective remedies to correct this failing. Hence, institutional response and political decision-making should aim at internalization of this negative externalities, inducing decision-makers (population) to respond to the consequences of their choices upon others just as if those consequences fell upon the decision-maker directly (Leitzel 2015). Inadequate internalization of such negative externalities might also materialize as a notorious "tragedy of commons." This "tragedy of the commons" concept, coined by Hardin (1968) and Gordon (1954), suggests that individuals might not see themselves as responsible for common resources such as public health and might eventually destroy such common resource (Demsetz 1967).

4 Nature, Scope, and Form of Regulation

Where market failures are accompanied by private law failures there is the prima facie case for regulatory intervention. However, does the mere existence of any market failures justify corrective government intervention? Many instances of market failures are remediable "by private law and thus by instruments which are compatible with the market system in the sense that collective action is not required" (Ogus 2004). Yet, as Professor Ogus (2004) convincingly shows private law cannot always provide an effective solution. Thus, where the "market failure" is accompanied with the "private law failure" there is, at least in theory, a *prima facie* (though not a conclusive) case for regulatory intervention. Namely, series of empirical studies have shown that the mere presence of suspected market imperfections does not by itself warrant government corrective action and regulatory intervention (Cheung 1973; Coase 1974). Namely, once the government steps in, it might often exclude private initiatives that might, in good entrepreneurial fashion, have invented ways of alleviating the suspected market imperfection (MacKaay 2015). "Government intervention tends to foreclose such demonstration and thereby to become a self-perpetuating process" (MacKaay 2015). Literature also suggests that even in instances of repeated market failures, the costs stemming from such imperfections should be weighed against those which government interventions itself generates (MacKaay 2015; Posner 2014; Ogus 2004). Namely, for such optimal governmental intervention one assumes perfect functioning of such public administration that merely maximizes social benefits.

However, governmental intervention, while seeking to address certain market failure (and maybe even effectively curing particular, individual market failure), may unintentionally while distorting the rests of the markets imposed even higher cost upon society and its citizens (Posner 2014). In other words, as a rule of thumb, regulatory intervention is warranted if, and only if the costs of such intervention do not exceed its benefits. The argument for such a rule of thumb is that either regulatory solution may be no more successful in correcting the inefficiencies than the market or private law, or that any efficiency gains to which it does give rise may be outweighed by increased transaction costs or misallocations created in other sectors of the economy (Ogus 2004; Viscusi et al. 1992; Kahn 1971).

The costs of government failure should be carefully compared and weighed against those of market failure. For example, such distortions may, besides government's tendency to perpetuate, materialize in rent-seeking activities of particular interest groups under the guise of the general interest.

Moreover, a traditional approach of political economy believed that it was the main function of the government to correct market failures (Towfigh and Petersen 2015). However, these justifications of governmental regulatory functions have one common weakness—they assume a perfectly functioning government. Yet, if there is a market failure, it cannot be excluded that there is also "government failure" (Towfigh and Petersen 2015). According to public choice theory one may assume that the main motivation of politicians is to maximize their individual utility and in principle seek to maximize the votes they get in a general election (Mueller 2003; Sunstein 1985). However, the regulatory intervention, enforcement of policies, and correction of market failures is in reality executed by the public administration (bureaucrats). Public choice theory suggests that also the bureaucrats' principal motivation is to maximize their utility (Tullock 1965; Downs 1967; Niskanen 1971). Their preferences often diverge, depending on the function that they exercise within the organization (Towfigh and Petersen 2015). Literature argues that they may be interested in job security, a higher salary, more attractive employment terms, an increase in power, public appreciation and status, or in decreasing their workload (Tullock 1965; Downs 1967; Niskanen 1971; Towfigh and Petersen 2015). Public choice theory hence suggests that bureaucrats are mainly motivated by maximizing their budget and might not be motivated, as assumed idealistically until the 1950s, by a romantic drive to correct market failures and other sources of inefficiencies.

In addition, poor policy may result from inadequate information, failure to anticipate significant side-effects of certain behaviour, phenomena (like super-intelligent AI), or regulatory instruments (Levine and Forrence 1990). Such poor regulatory intervention may occur where the government had to be seen to respond rapidly to widespread calls for action, following a disaster which had captured the public attention (Levine and Forrence 1990), or when it lacks resources or adapting a passive, compromising approach to contraventions (Cranston 1979;

Gunningham 1974). Therefore, public choice theory offers an additional support to our rule of thumb stating that "state interventions are only justified if they produce less harm than market inefficiencies."

5 Conclusion

In the previous chapter, we examined the law and economics methodology and comparative economic framework employed in this book. In this chapter, we considered the limitations of the "invisible hand" (forces of the "free" market) and explore the nature, scope, and limitations of regulatory intervention. This chapter also offers a brief list of public and private interest goals which might be the driving force behind regulatory activity, showing that public interest goals might vary according to time, place, and the specific values. Moreover, this discusses a crucial issue in the law and economics debates and also in other social sciences concerning the balance between the state and the market. We illustrated the operation of the perfect market, investigated the materialization of market imperfections (negative externalities and information asymmetries), introduced the concept of "government failure," and offered a regulatory rule of thumb suggesting that "state interventions are only justified if and only if they produce less harm than market inefficiencies." Namely, as this chapter emphasizes, if there is a "market failure," it cannot be excluded that there is also "government failure."

Bibliography

Acemoglu, Daron, and James A. Robinson. 2019. *The Narrow Corridor: States, Societies, and the Fate of Liberty*. New York: Penguin Press.

Akerloff, A. George. 1970. The Market for Lemons: Quality, Uncertainty and the Market Mechanism. *Quarterly Journal of Economics* 84: 488.

Arrow, J. Kenneth, and Gerard Debreu. 1954. Existence of a Competitive Equilibrium for a Competitive Economy. *Econometrica* 22: 265–290.

Baird, G. Douglas, H. Robert Gertner, and C. Randal Picker. 2003. *Game Theory and the Law*, 6th ed. Cambridge: Harvard University Press.

Cheung, N. Steven. 1973. The Fable of the Bees: An Economic Investigation. *Journal of Law and Economics* 16 (2): 11–33.

Coase, H. Ronald. 1937. The Nature of the Firm. *Economica* 4: 386.

Coase, H. Ronald. 1959. The Federal Communications Commission. *Journal of Law and Economics* 2 (1): 1–40.

Coase, H. Ronald. 1960. The Problem of Social Cost. *Journal of Law and Economics* 3 (2): 1–44.

Coase, H. Ronald. 1974. The Lighthouse in Economics. *Journal of Law and Economics* 17 (1): 357–376.

Cooter, Robert, and Thomas Ulen. 2016. *Law and Economics*, 7th ed. Hoboken, NJ: Pearson.

Cranston, Ross. 1979. *Regulating Business-Law and Consumer Agencies.* London: Palgrave MacMillan.

De Geest, Gerrit, and Mitja Kovac. 2009. The Formation of Contracts in the Draft Common Frame of Reference. *European Review of Private Law* 17: 113–132.

Delebecque, Phill. 1991. Contrat de renseignement. *J.-Cl. Contrats et Distribution, Fasc.* 795.

Demsetz, Harold. 1967. Toward a Theory of Property Rights. *American Economic Review* 57 (1): 347–359.

Downs, Anthony. 1967. *Inside Bureaucracy.* Boston: Little, Brown and Company.

Gordon, H. Scott. 1954. The Economic theory of a Common-Property Resource: The Fishery. *Journal of Political Economy* 62 (2).

Grossman, J. Sanford. 1981. The Informational Role of Warranties and Private Disclosure About Product Quality. *Journal of Law and Economics* 24 (1): 461–489.

Gunningham, Neil. 1974. *Pollution, Social Interest and the Law.* Hoboken, NJ: Wiley-Blackwell.

Hardin, Garrett. 1968. The Tragedy of the Commons. *Science* 162: 1243–1248.

Hirshleifer, Jack. 1984. *Price Theory and Applications*, 3rd ed. Cambridge: Cambridge University Press.

Hirschleifer, Jack, and John G. Riley. 1995. The Analytics of Uncertainty and Information. 3rd reprint, Cambridge: Cambridge University Press.

Hirschleifer, Jack. 1995. Where Are We in the Theory of Information. In *The Economics of Information*, eds. David K. Levine, and Steven A. Lippman, vol. I. Cheltenham: Edward Elgar.

Kahn, E. Alfred. 1971. *The Economics of Regulation: Principles and Institutions.* Cambridge: MIT Press.

Koopmans, C. Tjalling, and John M. Monthias. 1971. On the Description and Comparison of Economic Systems. *Cowles Foundation Paper, No. 357*, New Haven: Cowles Foundation for Research in Economics.

Leitzel, Jim. 2015. *Concepts in Law and Economics: A Guide for the Curious.* New York: Oxford University Press.

Levine, E. Michael, and Jennifer L. Forrence. 1990. Regulatory Capture, Public Interest, and the Public Agenda: Towards a Synthesis. *Journal of Law Economics and Organization* 6 (4): 167–191.

MacKaay, Ejan. 2015. *Law and Economics for Civil Law Systems*. Cheltenham: Edward Elgar.
Mackaay, Ejan. 1982. *Economics of Information and Law*. Boston: Kluwer Nijhoff Publishing.
Milgrom, R. Paul. 1981. Good News and Bad News: Representation Theorems and Applications. *Bell Journal of Economics* 12: 380–391.
Matthews, Steve, and Andrew Postlewaite. 1985. Quality Testing and Disclosure. *The Rand Journal of Economics* 16 (3): 328–340.
Miller, L. Roger, Daniel K. Benjamin, and Douglas C. North. 2017. *The Economics of Public Policy Issues*, 20th ed. Hoboken, NJ: Pearson.
Morell, Alexander. 2015. Demand, Supply and Markets. In *Economic Methods for Lawyers*, ed. Emanuel V. Towigh and Niels Petersen, 32–61. Cheltenham: Edward Elgar.
Mueller, C. Dennis. 2003. *Public Choice III*. Cambridge: Cambridge University Press.
Nicholson, Walter, and Christopher Snyder. 2008. *Microeconomic Theory*, 10th ed. Mason: Thomson.
Niskanen, A. William. 1971. *Bureaucracy and Representative Government*. Chicago: Aldine.
Ogus, Anthony. 2004. *Regulation: Legal Form and Economic Theory*. London: Hart Publishing.
Palandt, Otto. 2002. *Beck'sche Kurz-Kommentare Band 7, Palandt Bürgerliches Gesetzbuch*. Band 7, 61st ed., §675. Munich: Beck.
Pigou, C. Arthur. 1932. *The Economics of Welfare*. London: Macmillan.
Pindyck, Robert, and Daniel Rubinfeld. 2018. *Microeconomics*, 9th ed. Hoboken, NJ: Pearson.
Pinna, Andrea. 2003. *The Obligations to Inform and to Advise—A Contribution to the Development of European Contract Law*. Den Haag: Boom Juridische Uitgevers.
Posner, A. Richard. 2014. *Economic Analysis of Law*, 9th ed. New York: Wolters Kluwer.
Samuelson, A. Paul. 1947. *Foundations of Economic Analysis*. New York: Atheneum.
Schwartz, Alan, and Robert E. Scott. 2007. Precontractual Liability and Preliminary Agreements. *Harvard Law Review* 120 (3): 661–707.
Smith, Adam. 1776 (1937). *An Inquiry into the Nature and Causes of the Wealth of Nations*. New York: The Modern Library.
Smith Barrett, Nancy. 1974. *The Theory of Microeconomic Policy*. D.C. Heath and Cy: Lexington, MA.
Spence, Michael. 1973. Job Market Signalling. *Quarterly Journal of Economics* 87 (3): 355–374.

Spence, Michael. 1974. *Market Signalling: Informational Transfer in Hiring and Related Screening Processes*. Cambridge: Harvard University Press.

Sunstein, R. Cass. 1985. Interest Groups in American Public Law. *Stanford Law Review* 38 (29): 3829–3887.

Stigler, J. George. 1961. The Economics of Information. *Journal of Political Economy* 69 (3): 213–225.

Theil, Henri. 1967. *Economics and Information Theory*. Amsterdam: North-Holland.

Towfigh, V. Emanuel, and Niels Petersen. 2015. Public and Social Choice Theory. In *Economic Methods for Lawyers*, ed. Emanuel V. Towfigh and Niels Petersen, 121–146. Cheltenham: Edward Elgar.

Tullock, Gordon. 1965. *The Politics of Bureaucracy*. Washington, DC: Public Affairs Press.

Varian, R. Hal. 2010. *Intermediate Microeconomics: A Modern Approach*, 8th ed. New York: Norton.

Viscusi, W. Kip. 1992. The Value of Risks to Life and Health. *Journal of Economic Literature* 31 (4): 1912–1946.

Viscusi, W. Kip. 2007. Regulation of Health, Safety and Environmental Risks. In *Handbook of Law and Economics*, eds. Mitchell A. Polinsky, and Steven Shavell, vol. 1, Amsterdam: North-Holland.

Viscusi, W. Kip, John M. Vernon, and Joseph E. Harrington. 1992. *Economics of Regulation and Antitrust*. Cambridge: MIT Press.

Wittman, Donald. 2006. *Economic Foundations of Law and Organization*. Cambridge: Cambridge University Press.

CHAPTER 4

Introduction to the Autonomous Artificial Intelligence Systems

Abstract This chapter attempts to explain the main concepts, definitions, and developments of the field of artificial intelligence. It addresses the issues of logic, probability, perception, learning, and action. This chapter examines the current "state of the art" of the artificial intelligence systems and its recent developments. Moreover, this chapter presents the artificial intelligence's conceptual foundations and discusses the issues of machine learning, uncertainty, reasoning, learning, and robotics.

Keywords Autonomous artificial intelligent systems · Developments · Machine learning · Uncertainty · Reasoning · Learning · Robotics

1 Introduction

In the previous two chapters we examined the law and economics methodology and the conceptual foundation of any regulatory intervention. In this chapter, we briefly explore the field of artificial intelligence. The field of artificial intelligence attempts not just to understand but also to build intelligent entities and is regarded as one of the newest fields in science and engineering. The name "artificial intelligence" (hereinafter AI) was coined in 1965 and it currently encompasses a huge variety of subfields, ranging from general (learning and perception) to the specific, such as playing chest, proving mathematical theorems, painting, driving

M. Kovač, *Judgement-Proof Robots and Artificial Intelligence*,
https://doi.org/10.1007/978-3-030-53644-2_4

vehicles, and diagnose diseases. The complete account of the AI field exceeds the scope of this chapter and can be found elsewhere (Russell and Norvig 2016). Yet, before we get into the law and economics discussion of judgement-proof problem, it is worth briefly looking at the main concepts and developments of the current AI field. Hence, this chapter provides a brief introduction of the history of machine learning and offers a synthesis of how current "state of the art" AI systems are structured. AI systems aspire through their structures to have the ability to process unstructured data, to extrapolate it, and to adapt and evolve in ways which are comparable to human beings.

Literature operates with at least four definitions of AI (thinking humanly, acting humanly, thinking rationally, and acting rationally) ranging from definitions that are concerned with "though process" to the ones that deal with "ideal performance" (Russell and Norvig 2016). Historically all four approaches to AI have been followed and resulted in an unprecedented technological progress encompassing the emergence of intelligent agents, return of neural networks, knowledge-based systems, employment of hidden Markov models (HMMs), data mining, Bayesian network formalisms allowing rigorous artificial reasoning, and artificial general intelligence (AGI).

However, some leading scientists have expressed discontent with the current progress of AI and argued that is should put less emphasis on creating improved versions of AI that is good at a specific task (McCarthy 2007; Minsky 2007). Instead, they believe that the field should turn its attention to the "human-level AI where machines can think, learn, and create (McCarthy 2007; Minsky 2007; Nilsson 1998; Beal and Winston 2009). Moreover, Goertzel and Pennachin (2007) advance the idea of artificial general intelligence (AGI) that looks for a universal algorithm for learning and acting in any environment.

2 A General Background and Key Concepts

Giving a machine the ability to learn, adapt, organize, or repair itself are among the oldest and most ambitious goals of computer science. The field of artificial intelligence dates back to 1956 where the field was officially born at the workshop organized by John McCarthy at the Dartmouth Summer Research Project on Artificial Intelligence (Nillson 2009; Stone et al. 2016). Strikingly, nearly every technique employed today was actually developed several years/decades ago by researchers in the United

States, Canada, Europe, and elsewhere (Nillson 2009; Stone et al. 2016). It was Alan Turing who wrote on the concept of machine intelligence in a seminal 1950 paper which focused on human intelligence as a benchmark for AI (Turing 1950). Turing (1950) coined the so-called "Turing test" as a benchmark for intelligence. Namely, if "a human could be fooled by a clever computer program into thinking that the machine they were talking to was in fact human, then the machine would have passed the intelligence benchmark" (Turing 1950). Turing suggests that a computer in order to pass his intelligence benchmark would need to possess the following capabilities: (a) natural language processing; (b) knowledge representation (to store what it knows); (c) automated reasoning (to employ stored information to answer questions and to draw new conclusions); and (d) machine learning (to adapt to new circumstances and to detect and extrapolate patterns; Turing 1950). In addition to pass the total Turing test, the computer needs (a) computer vision (to perceive objects) and (b) robotics to manipulate objects and move about (Turing 1950; Haugeland 1985; Russell and Norvig 2016). Moreover, Turing in his 1936 groundbreaking paper introduced the concept of "universality" which means that society does not need separate machines for machine translation, chess, speech understanding, supply chains: one machine does it all (Turing 1936). This paper actually defined the so-called "Turing machine" which is regarded as the basis for modern computer science (Russell 2019). Russell (2019) even argues that this Turing's paper introducing universality was one of the most important ever written. Turing actually described a computing device—"Turing machine"—that could accept as input the description of any other computing device, together with that second device's input, and, by simulating the operation of the second device on its input, produce the same output that the second device would have produced (Turing 1936; Russell 2019). Furthermore, Turing (1936) also introduced precise definitions for two new kinds of mathematical objects—machines and programs.

Yet, the father of modern AI is generally credited to Marvin Minsky who developed the first randomly wired neural network learning machine—SNARC—in 1952 (Minsky 1952, 1969). Marvin Minsky and Dean Edmonds, at that time students at Harvard University, actually built the first neural network computer in 1950. In 1972 Newell and Simon formulated the famous physical symbol system hypothesis, stating that "a physical symbol system has the necessary and sufficient means for general intelligent action" (Newell and Simon 1972).

In the mid-1980s, Bryson and Ho (1975) reintroduced the back-propagation learning and the algorithm has been applied to many learning problems (Rumelhart and McClelland 1986). In recent years the approaches based on HMMs have come to dominate the area (Russell and Norvig 2016). These HMMs are based on rigorous mathematical theory and they are generated by a process of training on a large corpus of real speech data. Russell and Norvig (2016) suggest that by employing improved methodology the field arrived at an understanding in which neural nets can now be compared with corresponding techniques from statistics, pattern recognition, and machine learning, and the most promising technique can be applied to each application. As a result, the so-called data mining technology has spawned a vigorous new industry (Nillson 2009; Russell and Norvig 2016). Data mining is the process of discovering patterns or extrapolating them from data. For example, an AI agent may detect supermarket purchasing habits by looking at consumer's typical shopping basket or may extrapolate a credit score. In addition, the Bayesian network formalism was invented to allow efficient representation of, and rigorous reasoning with uncertain knowledge (Pearl 1988; Cheeseman 1985). Such normative expert systems act rationally and do not try to imitate the though steps of human experts (Horwitz et al. 1988). For example, the Windows operating system includes several such normative diagnostic expert systems for correcting problems. Russell and Norvig (2016) report that similar gentle revolutions have occurred in robotics, computer vision, and knowledge representation.

From 1995 one witnesses the emergence of intelligent agents and researchers returned also to the "whole agent" problem and to the complete agent architecture (Newell 1994; Tambe et al. 1995). Namely, one of the most important environments for intelligent agents became the Internet and AI underlie many internet tools, such as search engines, recommender systems and web site aggregators (Nillson 2009; Russell and Norvig 2016). Interactive simulation environments constitute one of today's technologies, with applications in areas such as education, manufacturing, entertainment, and training. These environments, as Tambe et al. (1995) suggest, are also rich domains for building and investigating intelligent automated agents, with requirements for the integration of a variety of agent capabilities but without the costs and demands of low-level perceptual processing or robotic control. Tambe et al. (1995) aimed at developing humanlike, intelligent agents that can interact with each other, as well as with humans, in such virtual environments. Their target was already back in 1995 intelligent automated pilots for battlefield-simulation environments (Tambe et al. 1995). These dynamic, interactive, multi-agent environments posed interesting challenges for research on specialized agent capabilities as well as on the integration of these capabilities in the development of "complete" pilot agents (Tambe et al. 1995).

Moreover, AI has been also drawn into much closer contact with other fields, such as control theory and economics. For example, Russell and Norvig (2016) suggest that recent progress in the "control of robotic cars has derived from a mixture of approaches ranging from better sensors, control-theoretic integration of sensing, localization and mapping, as well as a degree of high-level planning."

3 Setting the Scene: Definitions, Concepts, and Research Trends

Curiously, there is no precise, straightforward, universally accepted definition of artificial intelligence or even a consensus definition of artificial intelligence. Calo (2015, 2017) for example argues that artificial intelligence is best understood as a set of techniques aimed at approximating some aspect of human or animal cognition using machines. Haugeland's (1985) and Winston's (1992) definition is concerned with thought process, whereas Nilsson (1998) and Poole et al. (1998) address behaviour and rationality of intelligent agents. This book employs a more useful definition provided by Nilsson (1998, 2010) which defines artificial intelligence as: "Artificial intelligence is that activity devoted to making machines intelligent, and intelligence is that quality that enables an entity to function appropriately and with foresight in its environment" (Nilsson 1998; 2010; Poole et al. 1998). Moreover, throughout this book the term artificial intelligence will denote the superhuman, super-intelligent autonomous artificial intelligence that is autonomous and has the capacity to self-learn, to interact, to take autonomous decisions, to develop emergent properties, to adapt its behaviour and actions to the environment, and has no life in the biological sense.

However, in recent years the AI field is shifting from simply building systems that are intelligent to building intelligent systems that are human-aware and trustworthy (Stone et al. 2016). Particularly, a set of techniques that are known as "machine learning," supported in part by cloud computing resources and widespread, web-based data gathering have propelled the field and have been the main source of excitement. Machine learning (hereinafter ML) refers to the capacity of a system to improve its performance at a task over time (Surden 2014). ML develops algorithms designed to be applied to datasets with the main areas of focus being prediction (regression), classification, and clustering or grouping tasks (e.g. recognizing patterns in datasets). Nowadays, ML is divided into two main branches: (a) unsupervised ML (involving finding clusters of observation that are similar in terms of their covariates—dimensionality reduction; also, matrix factorization, regularization, and neuro-networks) and (b) supervised ML (using a set of covariates (x) to predict an outcome (Y)) (Blei et al. 2003; Varian 2014; Mullainathan and Spiess 2017; Athey 2018). Moreover, there are a variety of techniques available for unsupervised learning, including *k*-means clustering, topic modelling, community detection methods (Blei et al. 2003) and there are variety of supervised ML methods, such as regularized regression—LASSO, ridge and elastic net, random forest, regression trees, support vector machines, neural nets, matrix factorization, and model averaging (Varian 2014; Mullainathan and Spiess 2017).

The output, as Athey (2018) points out, of a typical unsupervised ML model is a partition of the set of observations, where observations within each element of the partition are similar according to some metric or vector of probabilities that describe a mixture of groups that an observation might belong to. Athey (2018) and Gopalan et al. (2015) suggest that older methods such as principal components analysis can be used to reduce dimensionality, while modern methods include matrix factorization, regularization on the norm of a matrix, hierarchical Poisson factorization and neural networks. On the other hand supervised ML focuses on a setting where there are some labelled observations where both X and Y are observed and the goal is to predict outcome (Y) in an independent test set based on the realized values of X for each unit in the test set (Athey 2018). Athey (2018) emphasizes that the actual goal is to construct $\mu(x)$, which is an estimator of $\mu(x) = E\ (Y/X = x)$, in order to do a reliable job predicting the true values of Y in an independent dataset. Yet, in the case of classification, the goal is to accurately classify observations. Namely, the main estimation problem is, according to Athey (2018), how to estimate $\Pr\ (Y = k/X = x)$ for each of $k = 1, \ldots, K$ possible realizations of Y. Yet, observations are assumed to be independent and the joint distribution of X and Y in the training data set is the same as that in the test set (Athey 2018). One also has to note the so-called reinforcement learning where the AI learning systems are exposed to a competitive environment where they train themselves continuously using trial and error to try to find the best reward (Nilsson 2009). Such AI attempts to learn from past experience in order to refine and improve decisions outcomes (Nilsson 2009).

As Calo (2017) points out very often thus task involves recognizing patterns in datasets, although ML outputs can include everything from translating languages and diagnosing precancerous moles. Yet, observations are assumed to be independent and the joint distribution of X and Y in the training data set is the same as that in the test set (Calo 2016; Athey 2018). This ML has been propelled dramatically forward by "deep learning," technique (operating within ML), which is a form of adaptive artificial neural networks trained using a method called back propagation (Stone et al. 2018). Stone et al. (2018) also emphasize that this leap in the performance of information processing algorithms has been accompanied by significant progress in hardware technology for basic operations such as sensing, perception, and object recognition. Deep learning (hereinafter DL) leverages many-layered structures to extract features from enormous data sets in service of practical tasks requiring pattern recognition or use other techniques to similar effect. These trends in ML and DL now drive the "hot" areas of research encompassing large-scale machine learning, reinforcement learning, robotics, computer vision, natural language processing, collaborative systems, crowdsourcing and human computation, algorithmic game theory and computational social choice, internet of things, and neuromorphic computing.

Recently, there has also been a dramatic rise in the effectiveness and employment of artificial specific intelligence (ASI) that is based around a specific task or application (Intelligent automation—IA). Moreover, industry has developed image processing and tagging algorithms that analyse to get data or to perform transformations and the 3D environment processing that enables algorithm in a robot (CAV—connected and autonomous vehicle) to spatially understand its location and environment (Russell and Norvig 2016).

Over the next fifteen years, the scholars expect an increasing focus on developing systems that are human-aware, meaning that they specifically model, and are specifically designed for, the characteristics of the people with whom they are meant to interact, and to find new, creative ways to develop interactive and scalable ways to teach robots (Stone et al. 2018).

It has to be emphasized that the AI's development is most advanced within military, academia and the industry which leverages an unprecedented access to enormous computational power and voluminous data (Pearson 2017). Moreover, Iyenegar (2016) points out that as few as seven corporations (Google, Facebook, IBM, Amazon, Microsoft, Apple, and Baidu) hold AI capabilities vastly outstripping all other institutions and firms. Finally, Calo (2017) suggests that the legal distinction should be made between disembodied AI, which acquires, processes, and outputs information as data, and robotics or other cyber-physical systems, which leverage AI to act physically upon the world.

3.1 Intelligent and Logical Agents

Literature identifies an agent as anything that can be viewed as perceiving its environment through sensors and acting upon that environment through actuators. For example, a robotic agent might be equipped with cameras and infrared range finders for sensors and various motors for actuators (Mitchell 1997; Russell and Norvig 2016). The AI then designs an agent program that implements the agent function, the mapping from precepts to actions (Putterman 1994; Kirk 2004). Such agents will via learning be able to operate in initially unknown environments and to become more competent than its initial knowledge alone might allow (Kepkhart and Chess 2003). Simple reflex agents respond merely directly to percepts, whereas model-based reflex agents maintain internal state to track aspects of the world that are not evident in the current percept (Russell and Norvig 2016). Moreover, goal-based agents act to achieve their goals and utility-based agents try to maximize their own happiness and can improve their performance through learning (Buchanan et al. 1978; Russell and Norvig 2016).

Moreover, the human process of reasoning also inspired AI's approach to intelligence that is currently embodied in the "knowledge-based agents." The central component of such a knowledge-based agent is its knowledge base formed from a set of sentences and each sentence is expressed in a knowledge representation language—axiom (Russell and Nordig 2016). Such knowledge base agents do three things: (a) it tells the knowledge base what it perceives; (b) it asks the knowledge base what action it should perform; and (c) the agent program tells the knowledge base which action was chosen and the agent executes the action (Russell and Nordig 2016). The application of "knowledge-based agents" and application of propositional interference in the synthesis of computer hardware is currently a standard technique having many large-scale deployments (Nowick et al. 1993). For example, such knowledge-based agents have been used to detect a previously unknown vulnerability in the web browser user sign-on protocol (Armando et al. 2008).

3.2 Problem Solving and Reasoning

AI agents may need to deal with the uncertainty and an AI agent may never know for certain what state it is in or where it will end up after a sequence of actions. In order to address such an uncertainty AI scientists resorted to the Bayesian probabilistic reasoning that has been used medical diagnostics since the 1960s and was used not just to make diagnostics but also to impose further questions and tests (Bertsekas and Tsitsiklis 2008; Gorry et al. 1973). Already in the 1970s one system outperformed human experts in the diagnosis of abdominal illness (de Donbal et al. 1974; Lucas et al. 2004).

Moreover, AI field offered the Bayesian networks as another solution to the problem of uncertainty. Bayesian networks are well-developed representations for uncertain knowledge and play a role analogous to that of propositional logic for definite knowledge and provide a concise way to represent conditional independence relationship in the domain (Pearl 1988; Jensen 2007). Inference in Bayesian networks means computing the probability of distribution of a set of query variables, given a set of evidence variables (Russell and Nordig 2016). The exact inference algorithms then evaluate sums of products of conditional probabilities as efficiently as possible (Jensen 2007).

However, AI agents must be able to keep track of the current state (belief state) to the extent that their sensors allow (Russell and Nordig 2016). In other words, AI agents have to address the general problem of representing and reasoning about probabilistic temporal process. From the belief state and a transition model an AI agent can actually predict how the world might evolve in the next step (Bar-Shalom 1992). Furthermore, from the percepts observed and a sensor model, the AI agent can then even update the belief state and quantify the degree in elements of which states were likely or unlikely (Oh et al. 2009). In addition, a combination of utility theory and probability theory to yield a decision-theoretic AI agent enables such an agent to make rational decisions based on what it believes and what it wants (Russell and Nordig 2016). As

Russell and Nordig (2016) show such an AI agent "can make decisions in context in which uncertainty and conflicting goals leave logical agent with no way to decide: a goal-based agent has a binary distinction between good (goal) and bad (non-goal) states, while a decision-theoretic agent has a continuous measure of outcome quality." However, modern AI agent already solves even more complex sequential decisions problems in which an AI agent's utility depends on a sequence of decisions. Such a sequential decision problem solving incorporates utilities, uncertainty, and sensing, and includes search and planning problems as special cases (Metz 2016; Russell and Nordig 2016). Currently, AI agents are using knowledge about the world to make decisions even when the outcomes of an action are uncertain and the rewards for acting might not be reaped until many actions have passed.

4 Learning and Communicating

Inspired by neuroscience some of the earliest work attempted to create artificial neural networks which eventually after 1943 leading to the modern field of computational neuroscience. Namely, an agent is learning if it improves its performance on future tasks after making observations about the world (Cowan and Sharp 1988; Russell and Nordig 2016). In unsupervised learning the agent learns the patterns in the input even though no explicit feedback is supplied (clustering). For example, Russell and Noordig (2016) suggest that an AI taxi agent may gradually develop a "concept of good traffic days and bad traffic days without ever being given labelled examples of each by a teacher." In reinforcement learning the agent learns from a series of reinforcements (rewards or punishments). Here, Russell and Nordig (2016) offer an example of a lack of any tip at the end of the journey which informs the agent that it did something wrong. In supervised learning the agent observes some input or outputs and learns a function that maps from input to output (Bishop 1995).

Modern artificial neural networks aim to most closely model the functioning of the human brain via the simulation and contain all of the basic machine learning elements previously discussed. In the world of AI, scientists have attempted to replicate or model our human neocortex structures and their functionality by the use of neural networks (Bridle 1990; Hopfield 1982). Neural networks represent complex non-linear functions with a network of linear threshold units, where the back-propagation algorithm implements a gradient descent in parameter space to minimize the output error (Bishop 2007; Russell and Nordig 2016). AI neural networks are composed of artificial input called "neurons" which are virtual computing sells that activate a numeric value and then hand it off to another layer of the network, which then again applies algorithmic treatment and this is then repeated until the data has passed through the entire network and is finally outputted (Mitchell 1997; Bishop 2007). These neural networks come in a variety of flavours (e.g. regression neural networks) that are generally trained to analyse data on either a linear or non-linear regression basis (Bishop 1995; Vapnik 1998).

On the other hand, convolutional neural networks (CNNs) have a structure which is optimized for image recognition, whereas generative adversarial networks improve its applications by pitting one CNN against another (Mitchell 1997). However, the nonparametric models employ all the data to make each prediction, rather than trying to summarize the data first with a few parameters (Bishop 2007). Fascinating support vector machines find linear separators with maximum margin "to improve the generalization performance of the classifier, whereas Kernel methods implicitly transform the input data into a high-dimensional space where a linear separator may exist, even if the original data are non-separable" (Bishop 1995; Russell and Nordig 2016). Deep learning networks are varieties of artificial neural networks that employ vastly greater computing power, more recent algorithmic innovations and much bigger data sets (Bishop, 2007). Whereas "decision tree" is an AI model that processes data via a series of question "nodes" (Bishop 1995).

5 Robotics

Artificial intelligence (AI) and robotics, they are two separate fields of technology and engineering. However, when combined, you get an artificially intelligent robot where AI acts as the brain, and the robotics acts as the body to enable robots to walk, see, speak, smell, and more. Generally speaking, robotics is a branch of engineering/technology focused on constructing and operating robots. Robots are programmable machines that can autonomously or semi-autonomously carry out a certain task and are designed to replicate the actions and behaviours of living cretaures. Robots use sensors to interact with the physical world and are capable of movement but must be programmed to perform a task (Bekey 2008). Robots are defined as physical agents that perform tasks by manipulating the physical world and to do so they are equipped with effectors such as legs, wheels, joints, and grippers (Mason 2001; Russell and Nordig 2016). Robots are also equipped with sensors which allow them to perceive their environment. Russell and Nordig (2016) report that present-day robotics employs a diverse set of sensors, cameras and lasers to measure the environment, and gyroscopes and accelerometers to measure the robot's own motion.

Most of the robots fall into three primary categories: (a) manipulators; (b) mobile robots; and (c) mobile manipulators (Mason 2001). Manipulators are physically anchored to their workplace (e.g. in factory, hospital) and their motion usually involves a chain of controllable joints, enabling such robots to place their effectors in any position within the workplace (Bekey 2008; Russell and Norvig 2016). Mobile robots move around their environment using wheels and legs (e.g. delivering food in hospitals, moving containers, or unmanned vehicles). Mobile manipulators or humanoid robots mimic the human torso and can apply their effectors further afield than anchored manipulators can (Dudek and Jenkin 2000; Russell and Nordig 2016). The field of robotics also includes intelligent environments and multibody systems where robots cooperate.

Traditionally, robots have been employed in areas that require difficult human labour (industry, agriculture) and in transportation (e.g. autonomous helicopters, automatic wheelchairs, autonomous straddle carriers). Moreover, they have also been employed as robotic cars that will eventually free us from the need to pay attention to the road during our daily travels (Murphy 2000). Robots are also increasingly used in health care to assist surgeons with instrument placement when operating on organs as intricate as brains, hearts, and eyes (Bekey 2008). Robots have helped in cleaning up nuclear waste in Fukushima, Chernobyl, and Three Mile Island. They have also explored for us the most remotes places like Mars or deep ocean waters, and are assisting astronauts in deploying and retrieving satellites and in building International Space Station. Drones are used in military operations and robots even explore for us the craters of volcanos. Robots also offer personal services in performing our daily tasks and include autonomous vacuum cleaners, lawnmowers, and golf caddies (Mason 2001). Furthermore, robots have begun to conquer the entertainment and toy industry. Finally, robotics is also applied in human augmentation (Russell and Norvig 2016). Scientists have developed legged walking machines that can carry people around and that can make it easier for people to walk or move their arms by providing additional forces through extra-skeletal attachments. Some robots, as Russell and Norvig (2016) report, go even as far as replicating humans (at least at a very superficial level).

6 Conclusion

The technological progress in the field of AI is an unparallel one and we may argue that AI is currently one of the intellectually most exciting and progressive fields of research. The daily application of AI is numerous and currently encompasses robot vehicles, speech recognition, autonomous planning and scheduling, game playing, spam fighting, logistics planning, robotics, and machine translation. These are just a few examples of AI systems that exist today. For example, NASA's Remote Agent program has become the first on-board autonomous planning program to execute and control the scheduling of operations for a spacecraft (Jonsson et al. 2000). Everyday AI systems classify billions of messages as spam saving us from deleting 80 or 90% of messages, if not classified by AI (Goodman and Heckerman 2004). The AI called DART (Dynamic Analysis and Replanning Tool), for example, provides automated logistics planning and scheduling for transportation that in hours generates a plan that would take weeks with older methods (Cross and Walker 1994). Machine translation programs employ statistical models and translate different languages at ever increased rate of precision and accuracy. Those are just a few examples offered by classic literature that exist already for a decade and indeed this is not science fiction but pure science, mathematics, and engineering (Russell and Nordig 2016). Today millions of AI applications are embedded in the infrastructure of entire states, industries, services, and societies. AI is unleashing the fourth Industrial revolution, its potential efficiency and productivity gains are unprecedented and social wealth accelerating processes unmatched by previous human inventions.

Bibliography

Armando, Alessandro, Roberto Carbone, Luca Compagna, Jorge Cuellar, and Llanos Tobarra. 2008. Formal Analysis of SAML 2.0 Web Browser Single Sign-on for Google Apps. *FMSE '08: Proceedings 6th ACM Workshop on Formal Methods in Security Engineering*, 1–10.

Athey, Susan. 2018. The Impact of Machine Learning on Economics. In *The Economics of Artificial Intelligence: An Agenda*, National Bureau of Economic Research.

Bar-Shalom, Yaakov (ed.). 1992. *Multitarget-Multisensor Tracking: Advanced Application*. Miami: Artech House.

Beal, Jacob, and Patrick H. Winston. 2009. Guest Editors' Introduction: The New Frontier of Human-Level Artificial Intelligence. *IEEE Intelligent Systems* 24 (4): 21–23.

Bekey, George. 2008. *Robotics: State of the Art and Future Challenges*. London: Imperial College Press.

Bertsekas, P. Dimitri, and John N. Tsitsiklis. 2008. *Introduction to Probability*, 2nd ed. Cambridge: Athena Scientific.

Bishop, Christopher. 1995. *Neural Networks for Pattern Recognition*. Oxford: Oxford University Press.

Bishop, Christopher. 2007. *Pattern Recognition and Machine Learning*. New York: Springer.

Blei, M. David, Y. Ng. Andrew, and Michael I. Jordan. 2003. Latent Dirichlet Allocation. *Journal of Machine Learning Research* 3: 993–1022.

Bridle, S. John. 1990. Probabilistic Interpretation of Feedforward Classification Network Outputs, with Relationships to Statistical Pattern Recognition. In *Neurocomputing: Algorithms, Architectures and Applications*, ed. Soulie Fogelman and Jean Herault. New York: Springer.

Bryson, E. Arthur, and Yu-Chi Ho. 1975. *Applied Optimal Control, Optimization, Estimation, and Control*. New York: Wiley.

Buchanan, G. Bruce, Tom M. Mitchell, Reid G. Smith, and C.R. Johnson. 1978. Models of Learning Systems. In *Encyclopedia of Computer Science and Technology*, ed. J. Belzer, A.G. Holzman, and A. Kent, vol. 11. New York: Marcel Decker.

Calo, Ryan. 2015. Robotics and the Lessons of Cyberlaw. *California Law Review* 103: 513–563.

Calo, Ryan. 2016. Robots as Legal Metaphors. *Harvard Journal of Law & Technology* 30: 209–237.

Calo, Ryan. 2017. Artificial Intelligence Policy: A Primer and Roadmap. *UC Davis Law Review* 51: 399–435.

Cheeseman, Peter. 1985. In Defense of Probability. *Proceedings of the International Joint Conference on Artificial Intelligence*.

Cowan, D. Jack, and David H. Sharp. 1988. Neural Nets. *Quarterly Review of Biophysics* 21: 365–427.

Cross, E. Stephen, and Edward Walker. 1994. DART: Applying Knowledge Based Planning and Scheduling to Crisis Action Planning. In *Intelligent Scheduling*, ed. Monte Zweben and Mark S. Fox, 711–729. San Francisco: Morgan Kaufmann.

de Donbal, F. Tom, David J. Leaper, Jane C. Horrocks, and John R. Staniland. 1974. Human and Computer-Aided Diagnosis of Abdominal Pain: Further

Report with Emphasis on Performance of Clinicians. *British Medical Journal* 1 (2): 376–380.

Dudek, Gregory, and Michael Jenkin. 2000. *Computational Principles of Mobile Robotics*. Cambridge: Cambridge University Press.

Goertzel, Ben, and Cassio Pennachin. 2007. *Artificial General Intelligence*. New York: Springer.

Goodman, Joshua, and David Heckerman. 2004. Fighting Spam with Statistics. *Significance, the Magazine of the Royal Statistical Society* 1: 69–72.

Gopalan, Prem, Matthew J. Hoffman and D.M. Blei. 2015. Scalable Recommendation with Hierarchical Poisson Factorization. In *UAI*: 326–335.

Gorry, G. Anthony, Jerome P. Kassirer, Alvin Essig, and William B. Schwartz. 1973. Decision Analysis as the Basis for Computer-Aided Management of Acute Renal Failure. *American Journal of Medicine* 55 (4): 473–484.

Haugeland, John (ed.). 1985. *Artificial Intelligence: The Very Idea*. Cambridge: MIT Press.

Hopfield, J. John. 1982. Neural Networks and Physical Systems with Emergent Collective Computational Abilities. *PNAS* 79: 2554–2558.

Horwitz, Eric, John S. Breese, and Max Henrion. 1988. Decision Theory in Expert Systems and Artificial Intelligence. *International Journal of Approximate Reasoning* 2 (3): 247–302.

Iyenegar, Vinod. 2016. Why AI Consolidation Will Create the Worst Monopoly in U.S. History, *TechCrunch*.

Jensen Verner, Finn. 2007. *Bayesian Networks and Decision Graphs*. New York: Springer.

Jonsson, K. Ari, Paul H. Morris, Nicola Muscettola, Kanna Rajan, and Ben Smith. 2000. Planning in Interplanetary Space: Theory and Practice. *AIPS-00*: 177–186.

Kephart, O. Jeffrey, and David M. Chess. 2003. The Vision of Automatic Computing. *IEEE Computer* 36 (1): 41–50.

Kirk, E. Donald. 2004. *Optimal Control Theory: An Introduction*. London: Dover Books.

Lucas, J. Peter, Linda C. van der Gaag, and Ameen Abu-Hanna. 2004. Bayesian Networks in Biomedicine and Healthcare. *Artificial Intelligence in Medicine* 30 (3): 201–214.

Mason, T. Matthew. 2001. *Mechanics of Robotic Manipulation*. Cambridge: MIT Press.

McCarthy, John. 2007. From Here to Human-Level AI. *Artificial Intelligence* 171 (18): 1174–1182.

Metz, Cade. 2016. In a Huge Breakthrough, Google's AI Beats a Top Player at the Game of Go. *Wired*.

Minsky, Marvin. 1952. *A Neural-Analogue Calculator Based upon a Probability Model of Reinforcement*. Cambridge, MA: Harvard University Psychological Laboratories.

Minsky, Marvin. 1969. *Basic Mechanisms of the Epilepsies*. New York: Little, Brown.

Minsky, Marvin. 2007. *The Emotion Machine: Commonsense Thinking, Artificial Intelligence and the Future of the Human Mind*. New York: Simon & Schuster.

Mitchell, M. Tom. 1997. *Machine Learning*. New York: McGraw-Hill.

Mullainathan, Sendhil, and Jann Spiess. 2017. Machine Learning: An Applied Econometric Approach. *Journal of Economic Perspectives* 31 (2): 87–106.

Murphy, R. Robin. 2000. *Introduction to AI Robotics*. Cambridge: MIT Press.

Newell, Allen. 1994. *Unified Theories of Cognition*. Cambridge: Harvard University Press.

Newell, Allen, and Herbert A. Simon. 1972. *Human Problem Solving*. New York: Prentice-Hall.

Nilsson, J. Nils. 1998. *Artificial Intelligence: A New Synthesis*. San Francisco: Morgan Kaufman.

Nilsson, J. Nils. 2009. *The Quest for Artificial Intelligence: A History of Ideas and Achievement*. Cambridge: Cambridge University Press.

Nilsson, J. Nils. 2010. *The Quest for Artificial Intelligence: A History of Ideas and Achievements*. Cambridge: Cambridge University Press.

Nowick, M. Steven, Mark E. Dean, David Dill, and Mark Horowitz. 1993. The Design of a High-performance Cache Controller: A Case Study in Asynchronous Synthesis. *Integration: The VLSI Journal* 15 (3): 241–262.

Oh, Songhwai, Stuart Russell, and Shankar Sastry. 2009. Markov Chain Monte Carlo Data Association for Multi-target Tracking. *IEEE Transactions on Automatic Control* 54 (3): 481–497.

Pearl, Judea. 1988. *Probabilistic Reasoning in Intelligent Systems*. San Francisco: Morgan Kaufmann.

Pearson, Jordan. 2017. *Uber's AI Hub in Pittsburgh Gutted a University Lab—Now It's in Toronto*, Vice Motherboard. Available at https://www.vice.com/en_us/article/3dxkej/ubers-ai-hub-in-pittsburgh-gutted-a-university-lab-now-its-in-toronto.

Poole, David, Alan K. Mackworth, and Randy Goebel. 1998. *Computational Intelligence: A Logical Approach*. Oxford: Oxford University Press.

Puterman, L. Martin. 1994. *Markov Decision Processes: Discrete Stochastic Dynamic Programming*. New York: Wiley.

Rumelhart, E. David, and James L. McClelland. 1986. *Parallel Distributed Processing, Volume 1 Explorations in the Microstructure of Cognition: Foundations*. Cambridge: MIT Press.

Russell, Stuart. 2019. *Human Compatible: Artificial Intelligence and the Problem of Control*. London: Allen Lane.

Russell, Stuart, and Peter Norvig. 2016. *Artificial Intelligence: A Modern Approach*, 3rd ed. Harlow: Pearson.

Stone, Peter, Rodney Brooks, Erik Brynjolfsson, Ryan Calo, Oren Etzioni, Greg Hager, Julia Hirschberg, Shivaram Kalyanakrishnan, Ece Kamar, Sarit Kraus, Kevin Leyton-Brown, David Parkes, William Press, AnnaLee (Anno) Saxenian, Julie Shah, Milind Tambe, and Astro Teller. 2016. *Artificial Intelligence and Life in 2030*. Report of the 2015 study panel 50, Stanford University.

Stone, Peter, Rodney Brooks, Erik Brynjolfsson, Ryan Calo, Oren Etzioni, Greg Hager, Julia Hirschberg, Shivaram Kalyanakrishnan, Ece Kamar, Sarit Kraus, Kevin Leyton-Brown, David Parkes, William Press, AnnaLee (Anno) Saxenian, Julie Shah, Milind Tambe, and Astro Teller. 2018. *Artificial Intelligence and Life in 2030*. Report of the 2015 study panel 50, Stanford University.

Surden, Harry. 2014. Machine Learning and Law. *Washington Law Review* 89 (1): 87–115.

Tambe, Milind, Lewis W. Johnson, Randolph M. Jones, Frank Ross, John E. Laird, Paul S. Rosenbloom, and Karl Schwab. 1995. Intelligent Agents for Interactive Simulation Environments. *AI Magazine*, *16* (1).

Turing, M. Alan. 1936. On Computable Numbers, with Application to the Entscheidungsproblem, or Decision Problem. *Proceedings of the London Mathematical Society*, 2nd ser., 42: 230–265.

Turing, M. Alan. 1950. Computing Machinery and Intelligence. *Mind, New Series* 59 (236): 433–460.

Vapnik, N. Vladimir. 1998. *Statistical Learning Theory*. New York: Wiley.

Varian, R. Hall. 2014. Big Data: New Tricks for Econometrics. *The Journal of Economic Perspectives* 28 (3): 3–27.

Winston, H. Patrick. 1992. *Artificial Intelligence*, 3rd ed. New York: Addison-Wesley.

PART II

Judgement-Proof Superintelligent and Superhuman AI

CHAPTER 5

What Can Get Wrong?

Abstract The newest generation of super-intelligent AI agents learn to gang up and cooperate against humans, without communicating or being told to do so. Sophisticated autonomous AI agents even collude to raise prices instead of competing to create better deals and they do decide to gouge their customers and humans. This chapter shows that super-intelligent AI systems might be used toward undesirable ends, the use of AI systems might result in a loss of accountability and the ultimate, unregulated success of AI might mean the end of the human race. Moreover, this chapter also suggests that the main issue related to the super-intelligent AI is not their consciousness but rather their competence to cause harm and hazards.

Keywords Hazards · Inefficiencies · Superhuman AI · Sophisticated robots · Consciousness

1 Introduction

In the previous chapters, we examined the rational and irrational human decision-making framework, introduced the methodological concepts of utility and wealth maximization and optimal regulatory intervention. We also considered the concepts, definitions and developments of the field of artificial intelligence and robotics. We also discussed the AI's problem

M. Kovač, *Judgement-Proof Robots and Artificial Intelligence*,
https://doi.org/10.1007/978-3-030-53644-2_5

solving, communicating, reasoning, and decision-making processes. In this chapter, we turn our attention to the potential problems, hazards, and harmful consequences that super-intelligent AI might cause and how can things get wrong. Is it possible for machines to act intelligently in the way us humans do? If they do, would they have real conscious minds?

Indisputably humankind faces an era where superhuman and superintelligent autonomous artificial intelligence and sophisticated robots are unleashing a new industrial revolution which will profoundly change and transform the entire society or at least the major part of it. Whereas some marvel at the capacity of artificial intelligence (Metz 2016) the others seem to worry aloud that our species will mortally struggle with super-powerful artificial intelligence and that it will be humankind's "final invention" (Barrat 2013; Russell 2019). Barrat (2013) for example argues that artificial intelligence indeed helps choose what books you buy, what movies you see, it puts the "smart" in your smartphone, will soon drive our cars, is making most of the trades on Wall Street, and controls vital energy, water, and transportation infrastructure (Barrat 2013). However, this super-powerful artificial intelligence can also threaten our existence. He also argues that in as little as a decade, artificial intelligence could match and then surpass human intelligence (corporations and government agencies are actually pouring billions into achieving artificial intelligence's Holy Grail—human-level intelligence; Barrat 2013). However, once the AI will attain human intelligence it will also have survival drives much like our own. Humans may be than forced to compete with a rival more cunning, more powerful, and more alien than anyone can imagine (Barrat 2013).

Namely, recent enormous increase in computational capacity and access to data has led to unprecedented breakthroughs in artificial intelligence, specifically in machine learning which actually triggered the attention of policymakers on the both sides of the Atlantic (Stone et al. 2016). Artificial intelligence combines, for the first time, the promiscuity of data with the capacity to do physical harm. Superhuman artificial intelligence combined with robotic systems accomplish tasks in ways that cannot be anticipated in advance; and robots increasingly blur the line between person and instrument (Calo 2015, 2016).

However, it has to be emphasized that arguments presented in this chapter are not about a super-intelligent AI that is conscious, since no one working in the AI field is attempting to make machines conscious.

It is about competence to cause harm and hazards, and not consciousness, that matters. Namely, if one writes an algorithm that when running will form and carry out a plan which will result in significant damages to life or property, unforeseeable hazards or even in the destruction of a human race, then it is not about the AI's consciousness but about its competence and capacity. The later can in certain fields already exceed that of any human and may also cause uncontemplated hazards. Russell and Norvig (2016) offer an example of an improved AI's generalization and faster learning in balancing triple inverted pendulum is achieved by an algorithm that adaptively partitions the state space according to the observed variation in the reward or by using a continuous-state, non-linear function approximator such as neural network giving to the AI a feat far beyond the capabilities of most humans. Even more impressive is for example an autonomous helicopter performing for human pilots a very difficult "nose in circle" manoeuvre. AI applies reinforcement learning to helicopter flight and the helicopter is under control of Pegasus policy-research algorithm (Kim et al. 2004). AI helicopters' performance now far exceeds that of any expert human pilot using remote control.

2 Can AI Think and Act Intelligently?

The question "will AI be conscious, will it think and act intelligently" will not go away even though no one quite knows what consciousness means, nor how we would know that AI was conscious (even if it was). The assertion that machines could act as if they were intelligent is called the "weak AI hypothesis" and the assertion that machines are actually thinking is called the "strong AI hypothesis." Currently, the AI science focuses on rational behaviour (the same criterion as defined and employed in the classic economics and discussed in Chapter 2) and regards an AI agent as intelligent to the extent that what it does is likely to achieve what it wants, given what it has perceived. Basing AI's rational decisions on the maximization of expected utility is completely general and avoids many of the problems of purely goal-based approaches, such as conflicting goals and uncertain attainment. However, the problem is that although most of us have an intuitive feel for our own consciousness (though we cannot describe it accurately) we have no such direct knowledge that anyone else is conscious (Wilks 2019). Wilks (2019) suggests that AI scientists and philosophers have "tried over decades to map consciousness onto something they do understand—such as suggesting machine learning programs may capture the unconscious neural process of the brain, while logical reasoning captures our unconscious planning and actions." American psychologist Jaynes for example argues that consciousness does not automatically come with being "homo sapiens" (Jaynes 1976). He suggests that after language was developed humans could start to talk to themselves in their heads and this self-conversation became an essential part of what we now call consciousness. Jaynes while abandoning the assumption that consciousness is innate, explains it instead as a learned behaviour that "arises ... from language, and specifically from metaphor" (Jaynes 1976). Such argument implies that only humans are conscious since only we have a language. Computers, as shown in previous chapter, do not talk to themselves yet, but one can envisage how they might. Wilks (2019) argues that one of the key features of programming languages is that they could be used to express plans or processes that required no specification at all of how "lover level" languages would translate the LISP code and carry the appropriate actions out in binary code on an actual computer.

Moreover, it is not so implausible that in near future AI entity might indeed discuss with itself what it intended to do, weigh up options but will not have any idea at all how its machinery would actually carry them out (Wilks 2019). Buyers (2018) for example suggest that a "HAL 9000" sentient supercomputer will have a greater degree of autonomy, independent thought and when it is created is very likely to be imbued with some form of personhood. Such a human behaviour is making as effective as we are (since we are not consciously controlling how we breathe or digest) and, as Wilks (2019) suggest, if AI had such self-discussion and we would have evidence of it, then we might start the discussion on whether an AI agent is indeed conscious.

However, as already emphasized, almost no one working in the AI field is attempting to make machines conscious. It is about competence to cause harm and hazards, and not consciousness that matters. Thus, the triggering question that a law and economics scholars have to address in order to design timely and optimal policy respond is on the AI's competence to cause hazards rather than the mere consciousness of its acts.

One can merely speculate on the AI agent's competence to cause harm but undoubtedly, AI capacities are increasing daily and in 2017 Google brain, OpenAI, MIT and DeepMind for example announced that technicians had created AI software which could itself develop further AI software (Zoph and Lee 2017; Simonite 2017; Duan et al. 2016; Baker et al. 2017; Wang et al. 2017). Turner (2019) even suggests that companies, governments and individuals are currently working on processes which go far beyond what those have yet made public. Bostrom (2014) in his book "Superintelligence" contemplates a form of superintelligence which is so powerful that humanity has no chance of stopping it from destroying the entire universe. His "paperclip machine experiment" imagines an AI agent asked to make paperclips which decide to seize and consume all resources in existence, in its blind adherence to that goal (Bostrom 2014).

Saying all that, it is clear that AI agents can do many things as well as or even far better than humans, including such enterprises like making music or poetry or inventing new medicines that people believe require great human insight and understanding. However, this does not mean that AI agents are conscious and that they use insights and understanding in performing their tasks.

3 Risks of Developing Artificial Intelligence

Can for example AI agents learn to gang up and cooperate against humans, without communicating or being told to do so? Could AI agents collude to raise prices instead of competing to create better deals? Can AI agents for example decide to gouge their customers and returned to the original, high price—in a move reminiscent of when companies in the same industry fix their prices instead of trying to out-sell each other? Indeed, one of very realistic sources of hazards and welfare losses is the collusive behaviour of AI and its potential manipulation of entire markets. Namely, pricing algorithms are increasingly replacing human decision-making in real marketplaces and for example most of the current trading on the world's stock exchanges is actually run by sophisticated AI agents. Collusive behaviour of such AI agents might not just severely impede the operation of stock exchanges but may even lead to unprecedented welfare losses, collapses of entire markets, and uncontemplated losses. Calvano et al. (2019) investigate whether pricing algorithms powered by AI in controlled environments (computer simulations) might start to collude, form cartels and eventually manipulate the entire markets. Thus, one would ask whether pricing algorithms may "autonomously" learn to collude. The possibility arises because of the recent evolution of the software, from rule-based to reinforcement learning programs. The new programs, powered by AI, are indeed much more autonomous than their precursors. They can develop their pricing strategies from scratch, engaging in active experimentation and adapting to changing environments (Harrington 2018). In this learning process, they require little or no external guidance (Calvano et al. 2019). In the light of these developments, concerns have been voiced, by scholars and policymakers alike, that AI pricing algorithms may raise their prices above the competitive level in a coordinated fashion, even if they have not been specifically instructed to do so and even if they do not communicate with one another (Kühn and Tadelis 2018; Schwalbe 2018). This form of tacit collusion would defy current antitrust policy, which typically targets only explicit agreements among would-be competitors (Harrington 2018).

In order to examine whether AI might indeed manipulate markets Calvano et al. (2019) studied the interaction among a number of Q-learning algorithms in the context of a workhorse oligopoly model of price competition with Logit demand and constant marginal costs. Quite shockingly, they show that the algorithms consistently learn to charge supra-competitive prices, without communicating with each other (Calvano et al. 2019). Moreover, these high prices are then sustained by classical collusive strategies with a finite punishment phase followed by a gradual return to cooperation (Calvano et al. 2019). What Calvano et al. (2019) found is that the algorithms typically coordinate on prices that are somewhat below the monopoly level but substantially above the static Bertrand equilibrium. Insightfully, the strategies that support these outcomes crucially involve punishments of defections and such punishments are finite in duration, with a gradual return to the pre-deviation prices (Calvano et al. 2019). Calvano et al. (2019) also suggest that the algorithms learn these strategies purely by trial and error. They are not designed or instructed to collude, they do not communicate with one another, and they have no prior knowledge of the environment in which they operate. Furthermore, one has to emphasize that their findings are robust to asymmetries in cost or demand and to changes in the number of players (Calvano et al., 2019).

Their findings might be path-breaking since up until now computer scientists have been focusing merely upon outcomes and not on strategies (Waltman and Kaymak 2008) or even argued that such collusion is not very likely to occur (Schwalbe 2018). Yet, the classic law and economics literature suggests that the observation of supra-competitive prices is not, per se, genuine proof of collusion (Bergh van den 2017). In law and economics literature collusion is not simply a synonym of high prices but crucially involves "a reward-punishment scheme designed to provide the incentives for firms to consistently price above the competitive level" (Harrington 2018; Bergh van den 2017). The reward-punishment scheme ensures that the supra-competitive outcomes may be obtained in equilibrium and do not result from a failure to optimize (Bergh van den 2017). From the standpoint of social wealth maximization findings of Calvano and his colleagues should probably ring an alarm bell (also for the competition authorities). Namely, currently the prevalent approach to tacit collusion is relatively lenient, in part because tacit collusion among human decision-makers is regarded as extremely difficult to achieve (Harrington 2018). However, as Calvano et al. (2019) show such AI collusive practices are obtained in equilibrium.

Moreover, literature identifies six potential threats to society posed by AI and related technology: (a) people might lose their jobs to automation; (b) people might have too much (or too little) leisure time; (c) people might lose their sense of being unique; (d) AI systems might be used toward undesirable ends; (e) the use of AI systems might result in a loss of accountability; and (f) the success of AI might mean the end of the human race (Russell and Norvig 2016).

The possibility that AI agents might be used toward undesirable ends has now become a real world scenario and the autonomous AI agents are now a common place on the battlefield (Singer 2009). Employment of these AI "warriors" also implies that human decision-making is taken out and that AI "warriors" may end up taking decisions that lead to the killing of innocent civilians (Singer 2009; Russell and Norvig 2016). In addition, game theoretical insights suggest that mere possession of powerful AI "warriors" may give states and politicians overconfidence, resulting in more frequent wars and violence. The AI has also potential of massive surveillance and the loss of privacy might be even inevitable (Brin 1998).

The use of AI systems may also result in loss of accountability. For example, if monetary transactions are made on one's behalf by the intelligent agent, is one liable for the debts incurred? Would it be possible for an AI agent to own assets and perform electronic trades on its behalf? Our attention in the rest of this book will be devoted exactly to the questions of whether the use of AI systems might result in a loss of accountability, whether such loss will create perverse incentives and whether an *ex ante* regulatory intervention might prevent the apocalyptic scenario of the end of the human race.

4 AI Making Moral Choices and Independent Development

Stuart Russell in his bestseller "Human compatible" discusses the possibility that the success of AI might even mean the end of the human race (Russell 2019). They suggest that almost any technology has the potential to cause harm in the wrong hands, but with AI and robotics, we might be facing a new problem that the wrong hands might belong to the technology itself (Russell 2019). Russell (2019) also suggests that AI system might indeed poses a bigger risk than traditional software and identifies three potential risks.

First, AI agent's state estimation might be incorrect, causing it to do wrong thing. For example, a missile defence system might erroneously detect an attack and launch its missiles killing billions (Russell and Norvig 2016). Yet, such risk can be technically easily mitigated by designing a system with checks and balances so that single state estimation does not lead to disastrous consequences. Second, specifying the right utility function for an AI agent to maximize is not so easy. For example, one may build AI agents to be innately aggressive or they might emerge as the end product of aggressiveness inducing mechanism design (Russell and Norvig 2016). Third, a very serious scenario, is where the AI agent's system learning function may, as Russell (2019) and Good (1965) suggest, evolve in an independent development, into a system with unintended behaviour (making even moral, humanlike choices). Vinge (1993) even states that "within thirty years, we will have the technological means to create superhuman intelligence and shortly after, the human era will be ended." Yudkowsky (2008) suggests that in order to mitigate such a scenario one should design a friendly AI, whereas Russell and Norvig (2016) argue that the challenge is one of mechanism design and to give the systems utility functions that will remain friendly in the face of changes. Namely, AI agent might reason that for example "human brains are primitive compared to my powers, so it must be moral for me to kill humans, since humans find moral to kill annoying insects" (Russell and Norvig 2016).

Minsky suggests that an AI program "designed to solve the Riemann Hypothesis might end up taking over all the resources of Earth to build more powerful supercomputers to help achieve its goal" (Minsky 2006). Hence, even if you built an AI program to prove theorems and if you give it the capacity to learn and alter itself, you need safeguards. In other words, the question is how to provide incentives to developers and producers of AI agents and systems to design such a friendly AI.

5 Conclusion

The field of AI has developed and designed the AI systems in line with classic economics concepts of rationality and wealth maximization. In line with this rationality the current generation of AI agents are intelligent to the extent that what they do is likely to achieve what they want, given what they have perceived. Literature suggests that it seems very likely that a large-scale success in creating super-intelligent, human-level AI intelligence will change the lives of majority of humankind. As already emphasized one can merely speculate on the AI agent's competence to cause harm but undoubtedly, due to scientific breakthroughs AI capacities are increasing daily and are becoming increasingly powerful. As showed, the very nature of our societies will be changed and superhuman AI could threaten human autonomy, freedom, and survival. Such a super-intelligent AI that is developing independently without human supervision could cause unprecedented hazards and harm. Moreover, current AI agents can already coordinate their behaviour, behave strategically and for example employ punishments to achieve desired outcomes. These modern AI agents are actually self-learning and employ different strategies purely by trial and error (like we humans do). Shockingly, in order furthermore, they are not designed or instructed to collude, they do not communicate with one another, and they have no prior knowledge of the environment in which they operate. Shockingly, super-intelligent AI agents actually do learn to gang up and cooperate against humans, without communicating or being told to do so. Namely, sophisticated autonomous AI agents collude to raise prices instead of competing to create better deals and they do decide to gouge their customers and humans. Finally, this chapter shows that super-intelligent, self-learning AI systems might be used toward undesirable ends, the use of AI systems might result in a loss of accountability and the ultimate, unregulated success of AI might eventually mean the end of the human race.

Bibliography

Baker, Bowen, Otkrist Gupta, Nikhil Naik, and Ramesh Raskar. 2017. Designing Neural Network Architectures Using Reinforcement Learning. *Cornell University Library Research Paper*, 22 March.

Barrat, James. 2013. *Our Final Invention: Artificial Intelligence and the End of Human Era*. New York: Thomas Dunes Books – Macmillan Publishers.

Bergh van den, Roger. 2017. *Comparative Competition Law and Economics*. Cheltenham: Edward Elgar.

Bostrom, Nick. 2014. *Superintelligence*. Oxford: Oxford University Press.

Brin, David. 1998. *The Transparent Society*. New York: Perseus Books.

Buyers, John. 2018. *Artificial Intelligence: The Practical Legal Issues*. Somerset: Law Brief Publishing.

Calo, Ryan. 2015. Robotics and the Lessons of Cyberlaw. *California Law Review* 103: 513–563.

Calo, Ryan. 2016. Robots as Legal Metaphors. *Harvard Journal of Law & Technology* 30: 209–237.

Calo, Ryan. 2017. Artificial Intelligence Policy: A Primer and Roadmap. *UC Davis Law Review* 51: 399–435.

Calvano, Emilio, Giacomo Calzolari, Vincenzo Denicolo, and Sergio Pastorello. 2019. Artificial Intelligence, Algorithmic Pricing and Collusion. *Review of Industrial Organization Volume* 55: 155–171.

Duan, Yan, John Schulman, Xi Chen, Peter L. Bartlett, Ilya Sutskever, and Pieter Abbeel. 2016. RL2: Fast Reinforcement Learning Via Slow Reinforcement Learning. *Cornell University Library Research Paper*, 10 November.

Good. 1965. Speculations Concerning the First Ultra Intelligent Machine. In *Advances in Computers*, ed. Alt and Rubinoff, 31–88. New York: Academic Press.

Harrington, E. Joseph. 2018. Developing Competition Law for Collusion by Autonomous Artificial Agents. *Journal of Competition Law & Economics* 14 (3): 331–363.

Jaynes, Julian. 1976. *The Origin of Consciousness in the Breakdown of the Bicameral Mind*. Boston: Mariner Books.

Kim, J. Ng, Michael I. Jordan, and Shankar Sastry. 2004. Autonomous Helicopter Flight Via Reinforcement Learning. *Advances in Neural Information Processing Systems* 16: NIPS.

Kühn, Kai-Uwe, and Steve Tadelis. 2018. The Economics of Algorithmic Pricing: Is Collusion Really Inevitable? Working Paper.

Metz, Cade. 2016. In a Huge Breakthrough, Google's AI Beats a Top Player at the Game of Go. *Wired*.

Minsky, Marvin. 2006. *The Emotion Machine: Commonsense Thinking, Artificial Intelligence, and the Future of the Human Mind*. New York: Simon & Schuster.

Russell, Stuart. 2019. *Human Compatible*. London: Allen Lane.
Russell, Stuart, and Peter Norvig. 2016. *Artificial Intelligence: A Modern Approach*, 3rd ed. Harlow: Pearson.
Schwalbe, Ulrich. 2018. Algorithms, Machine Learning, and Collusion. *Journal of Competition Law & Economics* 14 (4): 568–607.
Simonite, Tom. 2017. AI Software Learns to Make AI Software. *MIT Technology Review*.
Singer, W. Peter. 2009. *Wired for War*. London: Penguin Press.
Stone, Peter, Rodney Brooks, Erik Brynjolfsson, Ryan Calo, Oren Etzioni, Greg Hager, Julia Hirschberg, Shivaram Kalyanakrishnan, Ece Kamar, Sarit Kraus, Kevin Leyton-Brown, David Parkes, William Press, AnnaLee (Anno) Saxenian, Julie Shah, Milind Tambe, and Astro Teller. 2016. *Artificial Intelligence and Life in 2030*. Report of the 2015 study panel 50, Stanford University.
Turner, Jacob. 2019. *Robot Rules: Regulating Artificial Intelligence*. Cham: Palgrave Macmillan.
Vinge, Vernor. 1993. "The Coming Technological Singularity: How to Survive in the Post-human Era." *Vision-21 Symposium*. NASA Lewis Research Center and the Ohio Aerospace Institute.
Waltman, Ludo, and Uzay Kaymak. 2008. Q-learning Agents in a Cournot Oligopoly Model. *Journal of Economic Dynamics & Control* 32 (10): 3275–3293.
Wang, X. Jane, Zeb Kurth-Nelson, Dhruva Tirumala, Hubert Soyer, Joel Z Leibo, Remi Munos, Charles Blundell, Dharshan Kumaran, and Matt Botvinick. 2017. Learning to Reinforcement Learn. *Cornell University Library Research Paper*, 23 January.
Wilks, Yorick. 2019. *Artificial Intelligence: Modern Magic or Dangerous Future?* London: Icon Books.
Yudkowsky, Eliezer. 2008. Artificial Intelligence as a Positive and Negative Factor in Global Risk. In *Global Catastrophic Risk*, ed. Nick Bostrom, and Milan M. Cirkovic. New York: Oxford University Press.
Zoph, Barret, and Quoc V. Lee. 2017. Neural Architecture Search with Reinforcement Learning. *Cornell University Library Research Paper*, 15 February.

CHAPTER 6

Judgement-proof Problem and Superhuman AI Agents

Abstract The law and economics literature identifies the "judgement-proof problem" as a standard argument in law-making discussions operationalizing policies, doctrines, and the rules. This chapter attempts to show that super-intelligent AI agent may cause harm to others but will, due to its judgement-proofness not be able to make victims whole for the harm incurred and might not have incentives for safety efforts created by standard tort law enforced through monetary sanctions. Moreover, the potential independent development and self-learning capacity of a super-intelligent AI agent might cause its de facto immunity from tort law's deterrence capacity and consequential externalization of the precaution costs. Furthermore, the prospect that superhuman AI agent might behave in ways designers or manufacturers did not expect (as shown in previous chapter this might be a very realistic scenario) challenges the prevailing assumption within tort law that courts only compensate for foreseeable injuries.

Keywords Judgement-proof problem · Superhuman AI · Tort law and economics · Harm · Liability

M. Kovač, *Judgement-Proof Robots and Artificial Intelligence*,
https://doi.org/10.1007/978-3-030-53644-2_6

1 Introduction

In the previous chapter, we examined whether super-intelligent AI agents learn to gang up and cooperate against humans, without communicating or being told to do so. We have also emphasized that the main issue related to the super-intelligent AI agents is not their consciousness but rather their competence to cause harm and hazards. As the proceeding sections demonstrate, super-intelligent AI agent might be able to perform more action than merely process information and might exert direct control over objects in the human environment. Somewhere out there are stock-trading AI agents, teachers-training AI agents, and economic-balancing AI agents that might be even self-aware. Such super-intelligent AI agents might then cause serious indirect or direct harm. For example, as shown in previous chapter high speed trading AI agents can destabilize stock market, fix prices, and even gauge against consumers. One can also contemplate cognitive radio systems (AI agents) that could interfere in emergency communications, may hold potential, alone or in combination, to cause serious damages. AI agents have already caused its first fatalities. In 2017 a Tesla Model S operating by AI agent crashed into a truck, killing its passenger (Corfield 2017); and in 2018, an Uber car driven by AI agent hit and killed a woman in Arizona (Levin and Wong 2018). Moreover, in 2017 Chatham House report concluded that militaries around the world were developing AI weapons capabilities "that could make them capable of undertaking tasks and missions on their own" (Cummings 2017). This implies that AI agents could be allowed to kill without human intervention (Simonite 2018).

In order to mitigate this potentially serious hazards and harms the combination of the *ex ante* regulatory intervention (regulatory standards) and *ex post* imposition of liability via tortious liability is at law-maker's disposal. In other words, the system of *ex ante* regulation and *ex post* sanctioning is designed to deter a future harmful behaviour. Such harmful behaviour analytically speaking represents negative externalities where costs of person's activity are not fully internalized and hence the level of person's activity (and harm) is sub-optimal. The optimal behaviour is achieved where 100% of costs and benefits are internalized. A negative externality arises when one person's decision impacts someone else where no institutional mechanism exists to induce the decision-maker to fully account for the spillover effect of their action or inaction (Leitzel 2015;

Viscusi 1992, 2007; Coase 1959; Pigou 1932). These negative externalities can also trigger market failures given that the generator of the externality incurs no cost for the harm they cause others, making them exercise inadequate self-restraint (Cooter and Ulen 2016; Miller et al. 2017; Hirshleifer 1984). In other words, the private cost for the person creating the negative externality is lower than the social cost, which is the sum of that private cost plus the costs incurred by third persons (Pigou 1932; MacKaay 2015). Corresponding legal tort and contract law rules are then some of the most effective remedies for correcting this failing. Hence, the institutional response should aim to internalize these negative externalities (harm), forcing decision-makers (the population) to respond to the impacts of their choices upon others as if they were felt by the decision-maker directly (Leitzel 2015). Tortious or contractual liability then, by assuming individual's rationality and wealth maximizing behaviour, acts as a sophisticated institution that alters (deters) individual's decision-making process and induces him to internalize the costs of his activity (to take optimal level of precaution and care).

However, the triggering question is how would a lawmaker modify the superhuman AI agent's incentive structure (behaviour) taking into account that it might not be responsive to the usual tort and contract law rational-based incentive mechanisms? Thus, failing to achieve deterrence and optimal amount of precaution. Namely, the potential independent development and self-learning capacity of a super-intelligent AI agent might cause its de facto immunity from tort law's deterrence capacity and consequential externalization of the precaution costs. Moreover, the prospect that superhuman AI agent might behave in ways designers or manufacturers did not expect (as shown in previous chapter this might be a very realistic scenario) challenges the prevailing assumption within tort law that courts only compensate for foreseeable injuries. Hence, would then courts simply refuse to find liability because defendant could not foresee the harm that the super-intelligent AI agent caused and assigned on the blameless victim? Or would than the strict product liability assigning liability to manufacturers be applied as an alternative remedy?

This chapter explores the triggering issue of the super-intelligent AI agent's responsibility for potential harm. Namely, if a super-intelligent AI agent were to cause harm who should be responsible? This chapter attempts to show that super-intelligent AI agent may cause harm to others but will not be able to make victims whole for the harm incurred and might not have incentives for safety efforts created by standard tort law enforced through monetary sanctions. These phenomena known in the law and economics literature as a "judgement-proof problem" is a standard argument (Shavell 1986) in law-making discussions operationalizing policies, doctrines, and the rules. The law and economics literature on the judgement-poof problem is vast and has been exploring effects, extent, and potential remedies to this unwelcome disturbance in the liability system (Ganuza and Gomez 2005a; Boyd and Ingberman 1994). This chapter suggests that the super-intelligent AI agents may due to different reasons (e.g. design failure or self-developed, self-learned capacity, lack of awareness of what harm is, or disregard of general human-perceived responsibility and good faith behaviour) be also judgement-proof and may thus lack any incentives to prevent harm from occurring.

In other words, judgement-proof characteristic of super-intelligent AI agents, while self-learning and evolving in manners unplanned by its designers, may generate unforeseeable losses where current tort and contract law regimes may fail to achieve optimal risk internalization, precaution, and deterrence of opportunism. In addition, the chapter examines current tort, criminal, and contract law liability rules that could be applied and investigates the causality issues of superhuman AI agents.

2 Low of Torts: Responsibility and Liability

In everyday life, we expose ourselves to risks, which is why modern societies have formed norms that set standards of behaviour that limit these risks and thus reduce the social costs of events causing losses. Economists describe forms of harm that are not covered by private agreements in the world of high transaction costs, as external effects or negative externalities. The economic purpose of liability for damages (tort) is to prepare the perpetrators of damages and the injured parties to bear the costs of damages caused by lack of protection or caution themselves. Indemnification internalizes these costs by obliging the claimant to recover damages to the injured party, thereby causing the potential infringer to bear the costs of the damages themselves, and is therefore motivated to reduce them to an effective level and also to invest at an effective level own safety (optimum level of prevention and caution). In economic terms, therefore, the liability institution internalizes the externalities caused by high transaction costs. Therefore, establishing liability is one of a number of strategic instruments for internalizing externalities that result from high transaction costs (for example, tax incentives, criminal laws, and security regulations).

Materialization of damages or tort is a wrongful act against individual or body corporate and his, her, or its property, which gives rise to a civil claim usually for damages, although other remedies are available (e.g. injunctions). However, strictly legally speaking, liability for damages, in addition to the conclusion of contracts, is in the civil law countries the second most important reason for the formation of obligations. An indemnity obligation is an obligation of the person to pay damages for which he is liable—to pay compensation to the person who suffered the damage. Liability arising in tort is not dependent upon existence of a contractual relationship and obligations in tort are not agreed to voluntarily like many contractual terms, rather, obligations in tort are imposed by the law (Kelly et al. 2014). Liability is generally based on fault, although there are exemptions, and it is the courts which develop the principles relating to standards of care and required conduct (Kelly et al. 2014). The existing liability frameworks which could conceivably apply to what we termed superhuman AI agent's generated consequences can be broken down (apart from contract law) into two distinct categories: negligence (tort) and strict liability under consumer protection legislation. These two categories will be throughout this chapter also in the focus of our examination.

In civil law countries, damage can be caused either because someone interferes with foreign benefits without being in a commercial relationship with the injured party or it can also occur because contractual parties breach contractual obligation they have against the other. In the first case, we are talking about a criminal offence (German "*deliktrecht*") that is causing damages to third party, and in the second, we are talking about a classic tort. For example, Article 1240 of the French Code Civil reads: "Any act whatever of man, which causes damage to another, obliges the one by whose *faute* it occurred, to compensate it" (Elischer 2017; Rowan 2017; Le Tourneau 2017). Subsequently, Article 1240 of the French Code Civil holds: "Everyone is liable for the damage he causes not only by his act, but also by his negligence or by his imprudence" (Le Tourneau 2017). These two very concise rules apply to all areas of liability, such as personal injury, nuisance, and deceit, for each of which for instance English law holds a separate tort (van Dam 2007).

At the same time, in the civil law countries all the following conditions must be met for the occurrence of an indemnity obligation so that the damage caused is the result of an adverse act for which one party is liable:

a. the occurrence of an inadmissible harmful fact
b. the occurrence of damage,
c. causal link between the harmful act and the harm, and
d. liability for damages (van Dam 2007).

Obviously, no liability for damages is possible without liability for damages, whereby liability for damages is based on: (a) the guilt or wrongful conduct of the person causing it (subjective liability); and (b) causality, on the link between a harmful fact and a particular activity or thing, which is that the harmful fact—the cause of the harm comes from a particular activity or thing (objective liability).

The traditional distinction in German law of tort is between "Verschuldenshaftung" and "Gefährdungshaftung" (Kötz and Wagner 2016). van Dam (2007) suggests that the later term means strict liability, whereas the former is referred to as fault liability. It has to be emphasized that the "verschuldenshaftung" includes liability for intentional as well as negligent conduct (Kötz and Wagner 2016). In English law the three main sources of liability are contracts, unjust enrichment, and torts (Clerk et al. 2000; Charlesworth and Percy 2001). A tort provides requirements for liability in a certain factual situation or field of application and it is quite common to speak about the "law of torts." In Buckley and Heuston (1996) a tort is classically described as "…a species of civil injury or wrong (…). A civil wrong is one which gives rise to civil proceedings – proceedings which have a s their purpose the enforcement of some right claimed by the plaintiff as against the defendant." The emphasis is on the procedural rights a tort provides (Goudkamp and Peel 2014). On the other hand, for American common law of tort, Dobbs et al. (2015) gives the following definition: "…a tort is conduct that amounts to a legal wrong and that causes harm for which courts will impose civil liability." van Dam (2007) suggests that American approach is more comparable to a continental approach while focusing on wrongful conduct.

The purpose of liability for damages is to recover damages (compensation) and to provide optimal incentives for further prevention of harm. In general, compensation for doing so eliminates, compensates for, or mitigates the adverse effects of the harmful fact for which liability is given. Property damage must be repaid in such a way that it is restored before the damage has occurred—restored in previous condition. However, if this establishment is not possible, the responsible person is obliged to pay monetary damages for the rest of the damage. In this case, the dwarf has the right to recover actual damages and also lost profits. The amount of damages does not take into account the amount of the damage, the level of fault, the material status of the responsible person, and other circumstances.

Within the law of torts or "*deliktrecht*" liability can arise in a number of different ways. Important categories for the purpose of this book include negligence, strict and product liability, and vicarious liability. Although a comprehensive overview exceeds the scope of this book and can be found elsewhere (van Dam 2007), we will briefly discuss each of them in turn.

In the common law of torts negligence is most important of all torts, since it is the one tort which is constantly developing in the light of social and economic change. The tort of negligence gives rights to persons which have suffered damage to themselves or their property, against a party who has failed to take reasonable care for those people's safety (Adams 2010). Adams (2010) suggests that negligence is the commonest tort claim and is relevant to the whole gamut of accidental injury situations (e.g. road accidents, illness, and injuries caused by workplace, conditions and harm arising through medical treatment). Negligence also plays an important part in product liability, since a person who suffers damage because of defects in a product, caused by the carelessness of the manufacturer or other party responsible for the state of the goods, may have a right to sue in negligence (Adams 2010; Goudkamp and Peel 2014). To be successful under English common law in a claim of negligence, the claimant must prove that: (a) the defendant owed the claimant a duty of care; (b) the defendant failed to perform that duty; and (c) as a result—causation and remoteness—the claimant suffered damage (Goudkamp and Peel 2014). The modern stage test for establishing whether the duty of care exists was quantified in *Anns v. Merton LBC* (AC 728, 1978) where Lord Wilberforce introduced a two-stage test, which was then in *Caparo Industries plc v. Dickman* (2WLR 358, 1990) elaborated into the three-stage test. This three-stage test for establishing a duty of care requires consideration of the following questions: (a) was the harm reasonably foreseeable; (b) was there a relationship of proximity between the defendant and the claimant; and (c) in all circumstances, it is just, fair and reasonable to impose a duty of care (Kelly et al. 2014; Goudkamp and Peel 2014).

In respect to foreseeability, the claimant must show that the defendant foresaw that damage would occur to the claimant or should have reasonably foreseen that damage would occur (e.g. *Donoughe v. Stevenson*, AC 56, 1932). If there is no foreseeability, there can be no duty (e.g. *Topp v. London Country Bus Ltd.*, 3 All ER 448, 1993). To sum up, for a claimant to succeed in negligence she must be able to prove that the defendant owed the claimant a duty of care in relation to the harm suffered; that the defendant breached the duty of care by failing to live up to the standard of care expect of her; and finally that the claimant suffered harm as a result of the breach of duty which is not regarded a seeing too remote a consequence of the defendant's activity (Kelly et al. 2014). Goudkamp and Peel (2014) suggest that causation and remoteness of damage are the shorthand names given to the final element of an action in negligence.

French tort law apart from causation and damage only requires a *faute* in order to establish liability (Le Tourneau 2017). French doctrine distinguishes two elements of *faute*: an objective element focusing on the conduct of wrongdoer, and a subjective element relating to his personal capacities (van Dam 2007). Either *faute* is considered to be the breach of a pre-existing obligation, or it is conduct that does not meet the standard of the good family father (Elischer 2017; Rowan 2017; Le Tourneau 2017; van Dam 2007). German BGB in Article 276 I describes "Verschulden" as either intention (*Vorsatz*) or negligence (*Fahrlässigkeit*). In both situations German law of torts tests tortfeasor's knowledge of the risk and his abilities to prevent it. Negligence (*Fahrlässigkeit*) cannot be established if it would not have been possible to recognize and to prevent the risk (Markesinins and Unberath 2002). The burden of proof in German law of torts as regards negligence is on the claimant, but if unlawfulness follows from the breach of safety duty (*Verkehrspflicht*) or the violation of a statutory rule, provided they prescribe the required conduct in a sufficiently specific way, the burden of proof is shifted to the defendant (van Dam 2007; Markesinins and Unberath 2002).

However, literature notes that there are number of disadvantages with such a liability framework (Buyers 2018). First, there are real difficulties in English tort law in claiming damages for pure economic loss. Second, the institution of "contributory negligence" can act as a defence to liability, if tortfeasor shows that the injured party should have known of the defect but negligently failed to recognise it or negligently used the product or failed to take account of its operating instructions (in such cases damages are reduced to take into account the injured party's negligence). Third, a voluntary assumption of risk implying that if the injured party knows of the defect she is less likely to use it and if she does, that usually breaks the causative chain between defect and damage (Buyers 2018).

Strict liability exists where a party is held liable regardless of their fault (*responsibilité sans faute, verschuldensunabhängiige Haftung*). Such liability standard abandons any mental requirements for liability (Hart 1958). In this sense strict liability is also referred to as objective liability (*responsabilité objective*) or risk liability (*Gefährdungshaftung*), which means that liability is to be established independent from the tortfeasor's conduct (Koch and Koziol 2002). However, as van Dam (2007) emphasizes, in practice a strict liability is far from a clear concept, since it can be considered as liability without negligence, but elements of negligence often play a role in rules of strict liability. Justifications for strict liability include to ensure that the victim is properly compensated, to encourage those engaged in dangerous activities to take precautions, and to place the costs of such activities on those who stand to benefit most (Honoré 1988; Stapleton 1994).

Product liability refers to a system of rules which establish who is liable when a given product causes harm. The focus is on defective status of a product, rather than individual's fault. Two most developed systems of product liability are the EU's Products Liability Directive of 1985 (Council Directive 85/374/EEC) and the US Restatement (Third) of Torts on Products Liability, 1997 (Shifton 2001). According to the EU Products Liability Directive a product is defective "when it does not provide the safety which a person is entitled to expect, taking all circumstances into account, including (a) the presentation of a product; (b) the use to which it could reasonable by expected that the product would be put; (c) the time when the product was put into circulation." Owen (2008) suggests that the US Third Restatement adopts a slightly more structured approach according to which defects subject to the regime must fall into at least one of three categories: (a) design; (b) instructions or warnings; and/or (c) manufacturing.

Finally, we have briefly to mention the concept of vicarious liability which denotes a situation where an employer (principal) can become liable for the tort of an employee (agent) if it is committed during the course of employment (agency relationship). As a general rule, vicarious liability arises out of the employer/employee relationships, yet it can be found also in the principal/agent even in the employer/independent contractor relationships (Kelly et al. 2014). Vicarious liability therefore is not a tort but is actually a concept to impose strict liability on a person who does not have primary liability, that is, who is not at fault (Kelly et al. 2014). In other words, one person is liable for the torts of another.

3 Tort Law and Economics

Tort law (the law of compensatory damages) defines the conditions under which a person is entitled to damage compensation if her claim is not based on a contractual obligation and encompasses all legal norms that concern the claim made be injured party against the tortfeasor. Economically speaking every reduction of an individual's utility level caused by a tortious act can be regarded as a damage (Schäfer 2000). Tort law rules aim at drawing a just and fair line between those noxious events that should lead to damage compensation and others for which the damage should lie where it falls. The economic analysis of tort law starts from the belief that a legal rule for liability and responsibility for damages will give incentives to potential parties in a situation where damages have been inflicted upon injured party to alter tortfeasor' behaviour (Posner 1972; Shavell 2004a; Epstein 2016). While discussing tort law issues one has to note that economists tend to place more emphasis on the deterrent function of tort law, with a principle derived from their model that it is more economically robust to remain uninjured than to seek compensation and restitution (Calabresi 1970). Layers on the other hand tend to attach more value to justice and compensation goals of tort law, to identify a wrongdoer, punish them, and to provide compensation to the victim (Faure and Pertain 2019).

A thorough overview of tort law and economics literature exceeds the limitations of this book and can be found elsewhere (Cooter and Ulen 2016; Posner 2014; Schäfer and Ott 2004). However, Calabresi (1970) introduced a fundamental distinction between primary, secondary, and tertiary accident costs. Primary costs are the costs of accident avoidance and the damage that finally occurs, secondary costs refer to the equitable loss-spreading, and tertiary costs are the costs of administering the legal system (Calabresi 1970; Faure and Pertain 2019). Tort law should give incentives to a reduction of total social costs of accidents (Posner 1972).

Moreover, it should be emphasized that tort law and economics literature traditionally addresses three broad aspects of tortious liability. The first is the assessment of its effects on incentives (both whether to engage in activities and how much care to exercise to reduce the risk when so doing)—analytically speaking tort law is thus an instrument that improves incentives (De Geest 2012); second concerns risk-bearing capacity and insurance and the third is its administrative expense comprising the costs of legal services, the value of litigants' time, and the operating costs of the courts (Shavell 2007). These three categories are then subjected to rigorous cost–benefit analysis that should yield the marginal conditions for an efficient outcome. Wittman (2006) for example argues that the key is to find liability rule where the equilibrium levels of prevention undertaken by the injurer and the victim coincide with the optimal levels.

However, it should be emphasized that even after a long debate on the economic effects of tort law there is still much disagreement as to the legitimate place of tort law in modern society. Should tort law be a comprehensive and expanding deterrence system, regulating securities' and other markets, old and new hazards and then be open to all kinds of legal innovations necessary for optimal deterrence? Or should its domain be more restricted to the classical cases and leave complicated risks and hazards to other social institutions—safety regulations (Schäfer 2000). This depends to a great extent on two factors, the availability of private insurance against hazards and the capacity of civil courts to obtain and process information (Schäfer 2000). Schäfer (2000) also argues that tort law has to play a predominant role in reducing primary accident costs if one takes the view that civil courts can handle most of the informational problems properly, and that regulatory agencies, even though better endowed to collect and process information, are often influenced by well-organized interest groups Yet, Schäfer (2000) also emphasizes that independent from potential informational constraints the tort system cannot be an efficient institution as long as reducing the scope of liability results in distortive incentive effects which are less costly than the resulting savings of costs of the judicial system and easier insurance coverage (Schäfer 2000). As the costs per case filed are very high in the tort system, alternative institutions like no-fault insurance schemes or *ex ante* safety regulation might be better suited to reduce the overall costs of accidents than tort liability (Dewees et al. 1996). Dewees et al. (1996) also argue that in such circumstances only empirical research can then find out which system or which combination of systems is best suited to reduce accident costs.

To sum up, law and economics describes harms that are outside private agreements as negative externalities and the economic function of tort law is to internalize these costs by making the injurer compensate the victim. When potential wrongdoers internalize the cost of the harm that they cause, they have incentives to invest in safety at the efficient level. Hence, "the economic essence of tort law is its use of liability to internalize negative externalities created by high transaction costs" (Cooter and Ulen 2016).

4 Legal Concept of Agency and Superhuman AI

The first major legal concept to be addressed in this chapter and that will be challenged by super-intelligent AI is the institution of "agency." Usually literature refers to a classic agent–principal relationship (which will be discussed in Sect. 6 of this chapter) where the principal appoints the agent, yet in this part we refer to legal subjects which hold rights and obligations in certain legal system. Generally, by stipulating legal agents legal systems also regulate their behaviour (Turner 2019). In this general legal sense, a "legal agent" is a subject which can control and change its behaviour and understand the legal consequences of its acts or omissions (Latour 2005). As Turner (2019) suggests legal agency requires knowledge of and engagement with the relevant norms and "the agency is not simply imbued on passive recipients." Rather it is an interactive process where all legal agents are subjects but not all subjects are agents (Hart 1972; Shapiro 2006). Namely, there are many types of legal subjects (human and non-human) legal agency is currently reserved only to humans. Literature suggests that advances in AI may undermine this monopoly and wonders whether super-intelligent AI should be also granted the status of legal agency (Turner 2019). As it will be argued in the rest of this book granting super-intelligent AI the status of legal agency is, from the law and economics perspective, at least dubious if not completely unnecessary and risky. In other words, this book will, while employing law and economics insights, show that AI should not be granted separate legal personality (see Chapter 7).

Currently, many legal systems around the world operate with the concept of "personhood" or "personality," which can be held by humans (natural persons) and non-human entities—legal persons (Brooks 2002;

Allgrove 2004; Turner 2019). It has to be noted that although legal personality takes different forms across legal systems, it only entails the status of subject and no agent (Bayern et al. 2017; Turner 2019). Legally speaking the crucial requirements for establishing agency is the ability to take one action rather the another, and to understand and interact with the legal system. Turner (2019), while discussing the issue of legal agency, suggests that "AI may meet all of those three requirements, independent of human input." Consequently, such a superhuman AI agent might indeed from doctrinal legal viewpoint be qualified for the status of legal agency.

5 Causation and Superhuman Artificial Intelligence

Liability is essentially a scalable concept which is based factually on the degree of legal responsibility society place on a person and on the concept of causality. The traditional view of causation in civil and common law countries is that events may be characterized as linked through relationships of cause and effect. This causation issue also represents the second fundamental legal principle challenged by super-intelligent AI agent.

According to the traditional legal theory the defendant must have caused the plaintiff's harm. Without causation, the wrongdoer is simply not liable in tort for harm. According to the traditional law the claimant must show that, "but for" the defendant's action, the damage would not have occurred. This idea of causation may seem simplistic, but this impression is misleading. As every student of law and economics knows causation is a notoriously difficult topic and the "cause" in tort law typically involves a negative externality created by interdependent utility or production function (Cooter and Ulen 2016). A problem arises when there is more than one possible cause of the injury or loss (negative externality). Multiple causes raise number of difficulties in negligence and the established rule is that the claimant must prove that the defendant's breach of duty materially contributed to the risk of injury (*Bonnington Castings Ltd v Wardlow*, AC 613, 1956; Kelly et al. 2014). Moreover, when there is a break in the chain of causation, the defendant will not be liable for damage caused after the break if this break in chain is caused either by natural event, act of a third party or act of the claimant (Kelly et al. 2014). Furthermore, non-layers have to be instructed that even where causation is established, the defendant will not necessarily be liable for all of the damage resulting from the breach. Namely, the test of reasonable foresight is applied even if the causality is established. The question here is whether the damage is of such kind as the reasonable man should have foreseen (Kelly et al. 2014). If the harm was not reasonably foreseeable then liability is not established (*Hughes v Lord Advocate*, AC 837, 1963). For example in *Doughty v Turner Manufacturing Co Ltd.* (1 QB 518, 1964) an asbestos cover was knocked into a bath of molten metal. This led to a chemical reaction, which was at that time unforeseeable. The molten metal erupted and burned the claimant, who was standing nearby, Court held that only burning by splashing was foreseeable and that burning by an unforeseen chemical reaction was not a variant of this (*Doughty v Turner Manufacturing Co Ltd.*, 1 QB 518, 1964). Thus, in law the deemed cause of event is not simply a question of objective fact but rather of policy and value judgements. Turner (2019) suggests that the key question in relation to AI is whether the relationships which we have to date treated as being causal can withstand the intervention of super-intelligent AI.

The degree to which a super-intelligent AI agent could in theory assume responsibility for its actions depends, from a philosophical perspective, on the extent to which it is aware of those actions (Buyers 2018). Literature suggests that until relatively recently, the question of whether or not an AI agent should be accountable and hence liable for its actions was neglected, since a machine was merely a tool of the person using or operating it (Buyers 2018). There was "absolutely no question of machines assuming a level of personal accountability or even personhood as they were incapable of autonomous or semi-autonomous action" (Buyers 2018). As we have seen in previous section this is also the way in which the law has evolved to deal with machine generated consequences. Moreover, sentient super-intelligent AI agents will very soon have a substantive degree of autonomy, self-learning capacity, independent reasoning (thought), and development (see Chapter 4) and as Buyers (2018) suggests the real conundrum for lawmakers is how to deal with liability consequences and with the causality problem. As shown, in order to establish liability, one needs to demonstrate that the person or thing caused relevant losses or damages (causality). Namely, existing causative liability in civil and common law countries suffice when machine functions can by and large be traced back to human design, programming, and language (Buyers 2018).

In modern AI systems and machine learning this is generally almost impossible to achieve especially in artificial neural networks where even scientists are unable to determine how or why a machine learning system has made a particular decision (Russell 2019). For example, when a test vehicle in autonomous mode killed a pedestrian in 2018, Uber explained that "emergency braking manoeuvres are not enabled while thee vehicle is under AI agent's control, to reduce the potential for erratic vehicle behaviour" (Coldewey 2018). Here, as Russell (2019) suggests the human designer's objective is clear—do not kill pedestrians—but the AI agent's policy implements it incorrectly. "Again, the objective is not represented in the agent: no autonomous vehicle today knows that people do not like to be killed" (Russell 2019). Namely, as already emphasized (see Chapter 3) in reinforcement learning the agent learns from a series of reinforcements (rewards or punishments). In supervised learning the agent observes some input or outputs and learns a function that maps from input to output (Bishop 1995). Moreover, modern artificial neural networks aim to most closely model the functioning of the human brain via the simulation and contain all of the basic machine learning elements. In the world of AI scientists have attempted to replicate or model our human neo-cortex structures and their functionality by use of neural networks (Bridle 1990; Hopfield 1982). Neural networks represent complex nonlinear functions with a network of linear threshold units, where the back-propagation algorithm implements a gradient descent in parameter space to minimize the output error (Bishop 2007; Russell and Norvig 2016). AI neural networks are then composed of artificial input called "neurons," which are virtual computing sells that activate a numeric value and then hand it off to another layer of the network, which then again applies algorithmic treatment and this is then repeated until the data has passed through the entire network and is finally outputted (Mitchell 1997; Bishop 2007).

Furthermore, the current AI systems do not provide self-reporting on why they make a certain decision. Such a reporting duty might be either senseless, since probabilistic Bayesian structures and artificial neural networks are very difficult to decipher or it is also questionable whether a decision is traceable from causative viewpoint (Buyers 2018). In additional, it may be doubtful to characterize any undesired learned behaviour adopted by an AI agent a subjectively wrong merely because such an action produced undesired results.

Finally, as emphasized the law of tortious liability relies on concepts of causality and foreseeability. Foreseeability criteria as Turner (2019) suggests is employed in establishing both the range of the potential claimants (was it foreseeable that this person would be harmed) and the recoverable harm (what type of damage was foreseeable). As shown in Chapters 3 and 4, the action of super-intelligent AI agents are likely to become increasingly unforeseeable and hence the classic tort law mechanism might, except at a very high level of abstraction and generality (Karnow 2015), become inadequate to deal with potential harm caused by AI agents. This also implies that current law of negligence is ill-suited to address the challenges that super-intelligent AI agents impose upon our societies.

6 Judgement-proof Problem

The third major legal concept to be challenged by super-intelligent AI agent is until now overlooked judgement-proof problem of AI tortfeasors that might completely undermine the economic function of tort law. The human-centred judgement-proof problem received an extensive law and economics treatment, yet the notion that also super-intelligent AI agents might be judgement-proof (as humans that created it) has been largely exempted from the law and economics debates and severely understudied. Namely, as already emphasized the economic purpose of tort liability is to induce injurers to internalize the costs of harms that they have inflicted upon others (to internalize negative externalities). Tort law internalizes these costs of these harms by making injurer, tortfeasor compensate the victim. When then potential wrongdoers internalize these costs of harm that they cause, they will then be induced to invest in safety at the efficient level, take precaution, restrain themselves from further hazardous activity, and consequently refrain from such harmful activity in the future. The economic essence of tort law and its main function is according to classic law and economics literature (Calabresi 1961; Calabresi and Melamed 1972; Shavell 1980; Posner 1982; Cooter and Ulen 2016) its use of liability to internalize externalities created by high transaction costs. In other words, tort law system should *ex ante* deter harmful behaviour and should *ex ante* provide incentives for an efficient level of precaution and mitigation of harms and hazards. Liability rules are hence designed to direct their attention towards ways of reducing damage caused. Means to this end can include prudence in concrete cases, limitation of the general level of damage-production activity, and scientific research into products and methods for producing less harm (MacKaay 2015).

However, what if the tortfeasors do not have any means to pay in full for the harm they cause or if the simply feel indifferent (they do not care if they will be found liable or not) to the potential liability? Would in such circumstances existing tort law system still provide its ex ante designed incentive structure inducing an optimal level of precaution and mitigation of damages? What is legal system is dealing with the disappearing defendant? This possibility that tortfeasors are not able to pay in full for the harm they cause is in the law and economics literature known as the judgement-proof problem.

A tortfeasor who cannot fully pay for the harms that is caused and for which she has been found legally liable is said to be "judgement-proof." Shavell (1986) and Summers (1983) coined the term "judgement-proof" in his path-breaking article on the judgement-proof problem where they showed that the existence of the judgement-proof problem seriously undermines the deterrence and insurance goals of tort law. He notes that judgement-proof parties do not have the appropriate incentive either to prevent accidents or to purchase liability insurance (Summers 1983; Shavell 1986). In other words, the judgement-proof problem is of substantial importance, since if the injurers are unable to pay fully for the harm they may cause, their incentives to engage in risky activities will be greater than otherwise. Summers (1983) also shows that the judgement-proof injurers tend to take too little precaution under strict liability, since the accident costs are only partially internalized. Hence, the judgement-proof problem reduces the effectiveness of tortious liability in combating risk and also lowers the inventive to purchase liability insurance (Shavell 2007).

Moreover, one should note that strict liability provides incentives for an optimal engagement in an activity if parties assets are enough to cover the harm they might cause, but their incentives will be inadequate if they are unable to pay for the harm (Shavell 1986; Ganuza and Gomez 2005b). Furthermore, Shavell (1986) argues that also under the negligence rule in situations that injurers are not induced to take optimal care, or there are errors in the negligence determinations that sometimes result in findings of negligence, then the existence of judgement-proof problem induces injurers to engage more frequently (sub-optimally) in the activity than they normally would.

Furthermore, when injurers are unable to pay all the harm, that they might cause, then also their incentives to take care tend to be suboptimal and the motive to purchase liability insurance is diminished too (Shavell 1986, 2007). Shavell (1986) offers an example of the injurer's problem of choosing care x under strict liability, when his assets are $y < h$ and where the injurer's problem is formulated as minimizing $x + p\ (x)\ y$; where injurer chooses $x(y)$ determined by $-p'\ (x)\ y = 1$ instead of $-p'\ (x)h = 1$, so that $x(y) < x^*$ (and the lower is y, the lower is $x(y)$). In such instance the injurer's wealth after spending on care would be $y-x$, and only this amount would be left to be paid in a judgement.

Namely, risk-averse injurers who may not be able to pay for the entire harm they cause will tend not to purchase full liability insurance or any at all (Shavell 1986; Huberman et al. 1983; Keeton and Kwerel 1984). Particularly, the nature and consequences of this judgement-proof's effect depend on whether liability insurers have information about the risk and hence link premiums to that risk (Shavell 1986). Consequently, reduction in the purchase of liability insurance tends to undesirably increase incentives to engage in the harmful activity (Shavell 1986). In addition, to the extent that liability insurance is purchased, the problem of excessive engagement in risky activities is mitigated; but the problem of inadequate levels of care could be exacerbated if insurers' ability to monitor care is imperfect (Shavell 1986).

Boyd and Ingberman (1997) extend this analysis to alternative precaution and accident technologies (pure probability, pure magnitude, and joint probability-magnitude technology) and suggest supracompensatory-punitive-damages as a potential remedy for the inefficiently low incentives to adopt precaution. They also conclude that extending liability to lenders of capital to a risky undertaking is increasing the probability of environmental accidents (Boyd and Ingberman 1997). De Geest and Dari-Mattiachi (2002) revisit the use of negligence rules, punitive damages, and under-compensation and show the superiority of average damages over punitive damages in the pure probability technology. They also show that strict liability induces optimal precaution above a high and intermediate threshold of assets and zero-magnitude-reducing (or sub-optimal) precaution otherwise (De Geest and Dari-Mattiachi 2002).

Others have extended initial analysis on legal policy regarding liability insurance (Jost 1996; Polborn 1998) and provided the optimal conditions for the combined use of liability insurance (Shavell 2000) and a minimum amount of assets to undertake a given activity (Shavell 2002, 2004b).

Picker on the other hand explored the extension of liability to lenders who contribute capital to activity resulting in external harm and concluded that such extension is actually increasing the probability of accidents (Pitchford 1995). Whereas Hiriart and Martimort (2010), and Boyer and Porrini (2004) analysed the extension of liability in a principal–agent setting and suggest that the extension of liability towards deep-pocket related third parties might have a beneficial effect. Hiriart and Martimor (2010) show that when an agent is protected by limited liability and bound by contract to a principal the level of safety care exerted by the agent is sub-optimal (non-observable). Increasing the wealth of the principal that can be seized upon an accident has no value when private transactions are regulated but might otherwise strictly improve welfare. They also show that an incomplete regulation supplemented by an *ex post* extended liability regime can sometime achieve the second best (Hiriart and Martimor 2010).

7 Judgement-proof Superhuman Artificial Intelligence

Previous section discussed the judgement-proof phenomena identified among humans. But, what if also the superhuman AI agents would be immune to the tort law incentive stream? Can also a super-intelligent AI agent, like us humans, be judgement-proof? Could the future development of independent, self-learning superhuman AI agents also reveal the "judgement-proof" characteristic of such AI agents? Can one extrapolate the human-centric concept of judgement-proof problem also upon super-intelligent AI agents?

In its original, narrow meaning of the concept human-centric judgement-proof problem relates to the fact that human tortfeasors are unable to pay fully for the harm they may cause and hence their incentives to engage in risky activities will be greater than otherwise. Even under strict liability their incentives will be still inadequate if they are unable to pay for the harm. This phenomenon then severely reduces the effectiveness of tort law system (liability for accidents and harms) and result in more risky activity, hazardous behaviour, and higher magnitudes of harm, because they will treat losses that they cause that exceed their assets as imposing liabilities only equal to their assets (Shavell 2004a). Tortfeasor's activity levels will tend to be socially excessive and they will contribute too much risk.

However, the judgement-proof problem could be also defined much broadly to include also a problem of dilution of incentives to reduce risk which materializes due to person's complete indifference to the *ex ante* possibility of being found liable by the legal system for harms done to others and complete indifference to the potential accident liability (the value of expected sanction equals zero). This problem of dilution of incentives (broad judgement-proof definition) is distinct from the problem that scholars and practitioners usually perceive as a "judgement-proof problem" which is generally identified with injurer's inability to pay fully for losses and victims' inability to obtain complete compensation (Huberman et al. 1983; Keeton and Kwerel 1984). Thus, in this book we employ a broad definition of a judgement-proof problem which encompasses all potential sources of dilution of incentives to reduce risk and not merely the narrow tortfeasor's inability to pay for the damages. Of course, there are many contexts in which inability for losses plausibly may lead to dulling of incentives to reduce risk and literature suggests that incentives will particularly likely to be diluted with respect to those actions that would serve primarily to lower the severity or likelihood of extremely large losses exceeding parties' assets (Shavell 2004a). Shavell (2004a) also argues that incentives problems are exacerbated if parties have the opportunity to shield assets, such as "when an individual puts his property in a relative's name or when a firm transfers assets to a holding company."

If one then employs both the narrow and broad meaning of the judgement-proof characteristic of humans and extrapolates them upon super-intelligent AI agents then indeed it could be argued that also super-intelligent AI agents might be (in near future) judgement-proof. Such a "judgement-proof-super-intelligent" AI agent will be simply unable to pay for the harm it may cause, since it will not have any resources, assets it can pay from (AI as a perfect example of the so-called "disappearing" defendant phenomena). Moreover, it will be also completely indifferent towards the *ex ante* possibility of being found liable by the human-imposed legal system for harms caused, and hence its incentives to engage in risky activities will be inadequate, suboptimal. For example, if we were to imprison the AI agent for non-payment or for caused harm, why would it care? The effectiveness of current human-related tort law system will be severely undermined and the classic tort law system will found itself under extreme pressure to reduce the level of harm.

If the super-intelligent AI agent will be unable (due to plethora of reasons) to pay for all the harm it may cause, its incentive to take care will tend to be diluted. Consider for example the super-intelligent AI agent's problem of choosing certain level of care (x) under strict liability, when its assets are zero ($y < h$). If we extrapolate Shavell's (1980, 1986, 2007) path-breaking work and employ his model on incentives to take care (Shavell 1986, 2007) upon AI agents then the actual super-intelligent AI agents' problem might indeed be formulated as minimizing $x + p(x)y\ x$ where the super-intelligent AI agent chooses $x(y)$ determined by $-p'(x)y = 1$ instead of $-p'(h) = 1$ (so that $x(y) < x^*$). Thus, if the y (super-intelligent AI agents' assets) is for example zero then also $x(y)$ (AI agent's level of care) decreases to zero. Moreover, it has to be emphasized that the identified judgement-proof implications remain robust and unchanged even if we enable super-intelligent AI agents to own financial assets.

Of course, one may argue that super-intelligent AI agents do not share our rational, self-interested, wealth maximizing behavioural standards, and decision-making processes, and that they lack our, human system of moral and ethical values. One could also argue that we humans could simply program the AI agents to understand current human-centred tort law system (and the entire set of accompanied incentive mechanisms) and by doing that also *ex ante* adjust their hazardous activity on the optimal level ($-p'(h) = 1$) and also take optimal amount of precaution. Yet, as shown in Chapters 4 and 5 super-intelligent AI is exceptional, since it makes moral choices and it develops independently regardless of the initial programming. Namely, as shown super-intelligent AI has (a) the capability to learn from data sets and develop in a manner unplanned by AI system's designers; and (b) the ability to themselves develop new and improved AI systems which are not mere replications of the original seed-program (Wang 2006, 2018). For example, although the initial human designer's objective would be very clear (do not kill pedestrian) but the super-intelligent AI agent might implement it completely incorrectly, since the objective might either not be represented in an AI agent or might contradict its own decision-making process. Hence, even if we would *ex ante* program the super-intelligent AI agents to respond efficiently to the human-centred tort law incentive mechanisms we may still witness super-intelligent AI agents that will, due to its autonomous self-development, feature judgement-proof characteristic.

Namely, Nilsson (2015) suggests that a machine learns whenever it changes its structure, program, or data, in such a manner that its expected future performance improves. Moreover, previously discussed forms of machine learning (Chapter 4) indicate AI's ability to develop independently from human input and to achieve complex goals. Yet, it has to be noted that Bertolini (2013) for example argues that robots are merely products and current applicable rules present a sufficient degree of elasticity to accommodate existing as well as reasonably foreseeable applications. However, programs which utilize techniques of machine learning are not directly controlled by humans in the way they operate, think, learn, decide, communicate, and solve problems. This ability not just to think, but to think differently from us, is according to Turner (2019) potentially one of the most beneficial features of AI. Silver et al. (2017) when experimenting with AlphaGo Zero and surpassed by unexpected moves and strategies stated that "these moments of creativity give us confidence that AI will be a multiplier for human ingenuity, helping us humans with our mission to solve some of the most important challenges humanity is facing." Yet, as Turner (2019) emphasizes, this indeed may be so, but with such creativity and unpredictability comes attendant dangers for humans, and challenges for our legal system.

The previously discussed technical features of the autonomous AI analytically imply that this super-intelligent autonomous AI and related liability discussion should actually be conceptualized as a severe judgement-proof problem (addressed in previous section). Namely, as have been previously shown the law and economics concept of judgement-poof problem informs that if injurers lack assets sufficient to pay for the losses their incentives to reduce risk will be inadequate (Shavell 1986). This book argues that the judgement-proof characteristics of super-intelligent AI agent might actually completely undermine the deterrence and insurance goals of tort law and result in excessive levels of harm and unprecedented hazards. Namely, the evolution of a super-intelligent AI agents and its capacity to develop characteristics and even some kind of "personhood" (and consequently also completely unexpected harmful consequences) never envisaged by its designer or producer might completely undermine the effectiveness of the classical human-centred strict liability and other tort law instruments. The tort law system of incentives was indeed designed by and for the world of humans and the puzzle is whether such human-centred system could be effective in/for the future world of omnipresent super-intelligent AI agents. Deterrence goal might then be corrupted irrespective of the liability rule since the judgement-proof super-intelligent AI agents (possessing autonomous "personhood" and in control of its own decision-making processes) will simply not internalize costs of the accident that they might cause.

Moreover, potential judgement-proof characteristic of the super-intelligent AI also implies that AI's activity levels will tend to be socially excessive and they will contribute to the excessive risk taking of the autonomous AI (Shavell 2004a; Pitchford 1998; Ringleb and Wiggins 1990). Hence, as law and economics suggests tortious liability (of any kind) will not furnish adequate incentives to alleviate the risk (also there will not be any incentives for AI to purchase insurance). In other words, the insurance goal will be undermined to the extent that the judgement-proof tortfeasor (super-intelligent AI agent of any kind) will not be able to compensate fully (or not at all) its victims. Moreover, as shown by Logue the first-party insurance markets will also not provide an adequate response/remedy (Logue 1994).

To sum up, as of result of this features the fundamental legal concepts of agency and causation are likely to be stretched to breaking point. Super-intelligent AI agents are also likely to be judgement-proof. The potential independent development and self-learning capacity of a super-intelligent AI agent might cause its de facto immunity from tort law's deterrence capacity and consequential externalization of the precaution costs. Moreover, the prospect that superhuman AI agent might behave in ways designers or manufacturers did not expect (as shown in previous chapter this might be a very realistic scenario) challenges the prevailing assumption within tort law that courts only compensate for foreseeable injuries. The chances are that if we manage to build super-intelligent AI agent with any degree of autonomy our legal system will be unprepared and unable to control them.

8 Conclusion

This chapter argues that "agency," "causation," and "judgement-proofness" are the three major legal concepts that will be challenged by super-intelligent AI agent. Namely, identified judgement-proof characteristic of super-intelligent, superhuman AI agents, while self-learning and evolving in manners unplanned by its designers, may generate unforeseeable losses where current human-centred tort regimes may fail to achieve optimal risk internalization, precaution, and deterrence of opportunism. This chapter attempts to show that superhuman AI agents might actually be, due to the complete dilution of its incentives to reduce the risk, immune to the existing tort law incentive stream and that super-intelligent AI agent might, as us humans, be also judgement-proof.

Moreover, as the chapter attempts to show also another two fundamental legal concepts of agency and causation are likely to be stretched to breaking point. Current tort law system might fail to achieve deterrence and optimal amount of precaution. As argued, the potential independent development and self-learning capacity of a super-intelligent AI agent might cause its de facto immunity from tort law's deterrence capacity and consequential externalization of the precaution costs. The prospect that superhuman AI agent might behave in ways designers or manufacturers did not expect (as shown in previous chapter this might be a very realistic scenario) actually challenges the prevailing assumption within tort law of causality and that courts only compensate for foreseeable injuries. The inadequacy of current human-centred tort law concepts might culminate in the complete ineffectiveness of current human-related tort law system. Such scenario implies that the goals of existing human-centred tort law will be severely compromised, and the classic tort law system will found itself under extreme pressure to reduce the level of harm.

Bibliography

Adams, Alix. 2010. *Law for Business Students*, 6th ed. London: Pearson.

Allgrove, Benjamin. 2004. *Legal Personality for Artificial Intelligence: Pragmatic Solution or Science Fiction*. Oxford: Oxford University Doctorate Dissertation.

Bayern, Shawn, Thomas Burri, Thomas D. Grant, Daniel M. Häusermann, Florian Möslein, and Richard Williams. 2017. Company Law and Autonomous Systems: A Blueprint for Lawyers, Entrepreneurs, and Regulators. *Hastings Science and Technology Law Journal* 9 (2): 135–161.

Bertolini, Andrea. 2013. Robots as Products: The Case for Realistic Analysis of Robotic Application and Liability Rules. *Law, Innovation and Technology* 5 (2): 214–247.

Bishop, Christopher. 1995. *Neural Networks for Pattern Recognition*. Oxford: Oxford University Press.

Bishop, Christopher. 2007. *Pattern Recognition and Machine Learning*. New York: Springer.

Boyd, James, and Daniel E. Ingberman. 1994. Noncompensatory Damages and Potential Insolvency. *The Journal of Legal Studies* 23 (2): 895–910.

Boyd, James, and Daniel E. Ingberman. 1997. The Search for Deep Pockets: Is Extended Liability Expensive Liability. *Journal of Law, Economics and Organization* 13 (1): 1427–1459.

Boyer, Marcel, and Donatella Porrini. 2004. Modelling the Choice between Regulation and Liability in Terms of Social Welfare. *The Canadian Journal of Economics / Revue Canadienne D'Economique* 37 (3): 590–612.

Bridle, S. John. 1990. Probabilistic Interpretation of Feedforward Classification Network Outputs, with Relationships to Statistical Pattern Recognition. In *Neurocomputing: Algorithms, Architectures and Applications*, ed. Soulie Fogelman and Jean Herault. New York: Springer.

Brooks, Rodney. 2002. *Robot: The Future of Flesh and Machines*. London: Allen Lane/Penguin Press.

Buckley, A. Richard, and Richard F. V. Heuston. 1996. *Salmond and Heuston on the Law of Torts*. London: Sweet & Maxwell.

Buyers, John. 2018. *Artificial Intelligence: The Practical Legal Issues*. Somerset: Law Brief Publishing.

Calabresi, Guido. 1961. Some Thoughts on Risk Distribution and the Law of Torts. *Yale Law Journal* 70: 499–553.

Calabresi, Guido. 1970. *The Costs of Accidents: A Legal and Economic Analysis*. New Haven: Yale University Press.

Calabresi, Guido, and Douglas A. Melamed. 1972. Property Rules, Liability Rules, and Inalienability: One View of the Cathedral. *Harvard Law Review* 85: 1089–1128.

Charlesworth, John, and Rodney A. Percy. 2001. *Charlesworth and Percy on Negligence*, 10th ed. London: Sweet & Maxwell.

Clerk, F. John, William H.B. Lindsell, and Reginald W.M. Dias. 2000. *Clerk and Lindsell on Torts*, 18th ed. London: Sweet & Maxwell.

Coase, H. Ronald. 1959. The Federal Communications Commission. *Journal of Law and Economics* 2 (1): 1–40.

Coase, H. Ronald. 1960. The Problem of Social Cost. *Journal of Law and Economics* 3 (2): 1–44.

Coldewey, Devin. 2018. Uber in Fatal Crash Detected Pedestrian but Had Emergency Breaking Disabled. *TechCrunch*, 24 May.

Cooter, Robert, and Thomas Ulen. 2016. *Law and Economics*, 6th ed. New York: Pearson.

Corfield, Gareth. 2017. Tesla Death Smash Probe: Neither Driver nor Autopilot Saw the Truck. *The Register*.

Cummings, L. Marry. 2017. Artificial Intelligence and the Future of Warfare. *Chatham House*.

De Geest, Gerrit. 2011. *Contract Law and Economics—Encyclopaedia of Law and Economics*, vol. 6, 2nd ed. Cheltenham: Edward Elgar.

De Geest, Gerrit. 2012. Who Should Be Immune from Tort Liability. *The Journal of Legal Studies* 41 (2): 291–319.

De Geest, Gerrit, and Giuseppe Dari-Mattiachi. 2002. An Analysis of the Judgement-proof Problem Under Different Tort Models. German Working Papers in Law and Economics.

De Geest, Gerrit, and Giuseppe Dari-Mattiachi. 2005. Soft Regulators, Tough Judges. George Mason Law & Economics Research Paper No. 03-56.

Dewees, N. Donald, David Duff, and Michael J. Trebilcock. 1996. *Exploring the Domain of Accident Law: Taking the Facts Seriously*. Oxford: Oxford University Press.

Dobbs, Dan, Paul Hayden, and Ellen Bublick. 2015. *Hornbook on Torts*, 2nd ed. New York: West Academic Publishing.

Elischer, David. 2017. Wrongfulness As a Prerequisite Giving Rise to Civil Liability in European Tort Systems. *Common Law Review*. Forthcoming. Available at SSRN https://ssrn.com/abstract=2934912 or https://doi.org/10.2139/ssrn.2934912.

Epstein, A. Richard. 2016. From Common Law to Environmental Protection: How the Modern Environmental Movement Has Lost Its Way. *Supreme Court Economic Review* 23 (1): 141–167.

Faure, G. Michael, and Roy A. Pertain. 2019. *Environmental Law and Economics: Theory and Practice*. Cambridge: Cambridge University Press.

Ganuza, Juan Jose, and Fernando Gomez. 2005a. Being Soft on Tort: Optimal Negligence Rule Under Limited Liability. UPF Working Paper.

Ganuza, Juan Jose, and Fernando Gomez. 2005b. Optimal Negligence Rule under Limited Liability. *SSRN Electronic Journal*.

Goudkamp, James, and Edwin Peel. 2014. *Winfield and Jolowicz on Tort*. London: Sweet & Maxwell.

Hart, L.A. Herbert. 1958. Legal Responsibility and Excuses. In *Determinism and Freedom in the Age of Modern Science*, ed. Sidney Hook. New York: New York University Press.

Hart, L.A. Herbert. 1972. *The Concept of Law*, 2nd ed. Oxford: Clarendon Press.

Hiriart, Yolande, and David Martimort. 2010. The Benefits of Extended Liability. *RAND Journal of Economics* 37 (3): 562–582.

Hirshleifer, Jack. 1984. *Price Theory and Applications*, 3rd ed. Cambridge: Cambridge University Press.

Honoré, Tony. 1988. Responsibility and Luck: The Moral Basis of Strict Liability. *Law Quarterly Review* 104: 530–553.

Hopfield, J. John. 1982. Neural Networks and Physical Systems with Emergent Collective Computational Abilities. *PNAS* 79: 2554–2558.

Huberman, Gur, David Mayers, and Clifford W. Smith. 1983. Optimal Insurance Policy Indemnity Schedules. *Bell Journal of Economics* 14 (2): 415–426.

Jost, J. Peter. 1996. Limited Liability and the Requirement to Purchase Insurance. *International Review of Law and Economics* 16 (2): 259–276.

Karnow, E.A. Curtis. 2015. The Application of Traditional Tort Theory to Embodied Machine Intelligence. In *Robot Law*, ed. Ryan Calo, Michael Froomkin, and Ian Kerr. Cheltenham: Edward Elgar.

Keeton, R. William, and Evan Kwerel. 1984. Externalities in Automobile Insurance and the Underinsured Driver Problem. *Journal of Law and Economics* 27 (1): 149–179.

Kelly, David, Ruby Hammer, and John Hendy. 2014. *Business Law*, 2nd ed. Oxon: Routledge.

Koch, A. Bernhard, and Helmut Koziol, eds. 2002. *Unification of Tort Law: Strict Liability*. The Hague, Boston, and London: Kluwer.

Kötz, Hein, and Gerhard Wagner. 2016. *Deliktsrecht*, 13th ed. Munich: Vahlen.

Latour, Bruno. 2005. *Reassembling the Social: An Introduction to Actor-Network Theory*. Oxford: Oxford University Press.

Leitzel, Jim. 2015. *Concepts in Law and Economics*. New York: Oxford University Press.

Le Tourneau, Philippe. 2017. *Droit de la Responsabilité et des Contrats - Régimes D'indemnisation 2018–2019*. Paris: Dalloz.

Levin, Sam, and Julia C. Wong. 2018. Self-driving Uber Kills Arizona Women in First Fatal Crash Involving Pedestrian. *The Guardian*.

Logue, D. Kyle. 1994. Solving the Judgement-proof Problem. *Texas Law Review* 72: 1375–1394.

MacKaay, Ejan. 2015. *Law and Economics for Civil Law Systems*. Cheltenham: Edward Elgar.

Markesinis, S. Basil, and Hannes Unberath. 2002. *The German Law of Torts: A Comparative Treatise*, 4th ed. Oxford: Hart Publishing.

Miller, L. Roger, Daniel K. Benjamin, and Douglas C. North. 2017. *The Economics of Public Policy Issues*, 20th ed. New York: Pearson.

Mitchell, M Tom. 1997. *Machine Learning*. New York: McGraw-Hill.

Nilsson, J. Nils. 2015. *Introduction to Machine Learning: Drafts of a Proposed Textbook*. Stanford University.

Owen, G. David. 2008. *Products Liability Law*, 2nd ed. St. Paul: Thomson West.

Pigou, C. Arthur. 1932. *The Economics of Welfare*. London: Macmillan.

Pitchford, Rohan. 1995. How Liable Should a Lender Be? The Case of Judgement-proof Firms and Environmental Risk. *American Economic Review* 85: 1171–1186.

Pitchford, Rohan. 1998. Judgement-proofness. In *The New Palgrave Dictionary of Economics and the Law*, ed. Peter Newman Peter, 380–383. London: Macmillan.

Polborn, Mattias. 1998. Mandatory Insurance and the Judgement-proof Problem. *International Review of Law and Economics* 18 (2): 141–146.

Posner, A. Richard. 1972. *Economic Analysis of Law*, 1st ed. Boston: Little, Brown and Company.

Posner, A. Richard. 1982. *Tort Law: Cases and Economic Analysis*. Boston: Little Brown.

Posner, A. Richard. 2014. *Economic Analysis of Law*, 9th ed. New York: Wolters Kluwer.

Ringleb, H. Al, and Steven N. Wiggins. 1990. Liability and Large-Scale, Long-Ter, Hazards. *Journal of Political Economy* 98: 574–595.

Rowan, Solène. 2017. The New French Law of Contract. *International and Comparative Law Quarterly* 66 (4): 805–831.

Russell, Stuart. 2019. *Human Compatible*. London: Allen Lane.

Russell, Stuart, and Peter Norvig. 2016. *Artificial Intelligence: A Modern Approach*, 3rd ed. Harlow: Pearson.

Schäfer, Hans-Bernd. 2000. Tort Law. In *Encyclopaedia of Law and Economics*, vol. II, ed. Gerrit De Geest and Boudewijn Bouckaert. Civil Law and Economics. Cheltenham: Edward Elgar.

Schäfer, Hans-Bernd, and Claus Ott. 2004. *The Economic Analysis of Civil Law*. Cheltenham: Edward Elgar.

Shapiro, J. Scott. 2006. What Is the Internal Point of View? *Fordham Law Review* 75: 1157–1170.

Shavell, M. Steven. 1980. Strict Liability Versus Negligence. *Journal of Legal Studies* 9 (1): 1–15.

Shavell, M. Steven. 1986. The Judgement Proof Problem. *International Review of Law and Economics* 6 (1): 45–58.

Shavell, M. Steven. 2000. On the Social Function and the Regulation of Liability Insurance. *Geneva Papers on Risk and Insurance, Issues and Practice* 25: 166–179.

Shavell, M. Steven. 2002. Minimum Assets Requirements. Working paper, John M. Olin Center for Law and Economics, and Business, Harvard Law School, Cambridge.

Shavell, M. Steven. 2004a. *Foundations of the Economics Analysis of Law*. Cambridge: Harvard University Press.

Shavell, M. Steven. 2004b. Minimum Assets Requirement and Compulsory Liability Insurance as Solutions to the Judgement-proof Problem. Working paper, John M. Olin Center for Law and Economics, and Business, Harvard Law School, Cambridge.

Shavell, M. Steven. 2007. Liability for Accidents. In *Handbook of Law and Economics*, vol. 1, ed. Mitchell A. Polinsky and Steven Shavell, 139–183. Amsterdam: North-Holland.

Shifton, Marc. 2001. The Restatement (Third) of Torts: Products Liability-The Aps Cure for Prescription Drug Design Liability. *Fordham Urban Law Journal* 29 (6): 2343–2386.

Silver, David, Julian Schrittwieser, Karen Simonyan, Ioannis Antonoglou, Aja Huang, Arthur Guez, Thomas Hubert, Lucas Baker, Matthew Lai, Adrian

Bolton, Yutian Chen, Timothy Lillicrap, Fan Hui, Laurent Sifre, George van den Driessche, Thore Graepel, and Demis Hassabis. 2017. Mastering the Game of Go Without Human Knowledge. *Nature* 550.
Simonite, Tom. 2018. Robotic Rampage' Unlikely Reason for Death. *New Scientist*.
Stapleton, Jane. 1994. *Product Liability*. London: Butterworths.
Summers, John. 1983. The Case of the Disappearing Defendant: An Economic Analysis. *University of Pennsylvania Law Review* 132: 145–185.
Turner, Jacob. 2019. *Robot Rules: Regulating Artificial Intelligence*. Cham: Palgrave Macmillan.
van Dam, Cees. 2007. *European Tort Law*. Oxford: Oxford University Press.
Viscusi, W. Kip. 1992. *Fatal Tradeoffs: Public and Private Responsibilities for Risk*. Oxford: Oxford University Press.
Viscusi, W. Kip. 2007. Regulation of Health, Safety and Environmental Risks. In *Handbook of Law and Economics*, vol. 1, ed. Michael Polinsky and Steven Shavell. New York: North-Holland.
Wang, Pei. 2006. *Rigid Flexibility: The Logic of Intelligence*. New York: Springer.
Wang, Pei. 2018. The Risk and Safety of AI. *NARS: An AGI Project*.
Wittman, Donald. 2006. *Economic Foundations of Law and Organization*. Cambridge: Cambridge University Press.

CHAPTER 7

Towards Optimal Regulatory Framework: Ex Ante Regulation of Risks and Hazards

Abstract The previous discussion on super-intelligent, humanlike self-learning characteristics of the autonomous AI agents and the extrapolation of the main findings of the law and economics literature upon such superhuman AI agents suggests that lawmakers are facing an unprecedented challenge of how to simultaneously regulate potential harmful and hazardous activity and how to keep incentives to innovate undistorted. This chapter attempts to offer a set of law and economics informed principles that might mitigate the identified shortcomings of the current human-centred tort law system. Moreover, this section offers a set of law and economics recommendations for an improved regulatory intervention which should deter judgement-proof super-intelligent AI agent's related hazards, induce optimal precaution, and simultaneously preserve dynamic efficiency—incentives to innovate undistorted.

Keywords Regulation · Regulatory sandboxes · Design timing · Vicarious liability · Tort law and economics

1 Introduction

In the previous chapter, we examined the potential "judgement-proof" characteristic of the super-intelligent AI agents, making such AI agent de facto immune from the existing incentive stream of the human-centred

M. Kovač, *Judgement-Proof Robots and Artificial Intelligence*,
https://doi.org/10.1007/978-3-030-53644-2_7

tort law system. Moreover, as shown in Chapter 4 super-intelligent AI agents might easily learn to gang up and cooperate against humans, without communicating or being told to do so. We have also emphasized that the main issue related to the super-intelligent AI agents is not their consciousness but rather their competence to cause harm and hazards. As the proceeding sections demonstrate, super-intelligent AI agents might be able to perform more action than merely process information and might exert direct control over objects in the human environment. Somewhere out there are stock-trading AI agents, teachers-training AI agents, and economic-balancing AI agents that might be even self-aware. Such super-intelligent AI agents might then cause serious indirect or direct harm. Yet, as shown in Chapter 5, current human-centred tort law regimes may indeed due to identified judgement-proofness and shortcomings of the current fundamental principles of foreseeability and causality (necessary tort law requirements for establishing liability), fail to achieve optimal risk internalization, precaution, and deterrence of opportunism. The goals of existing human-centred tort law might be severely compromised, and the classic tort law system might found itself under extreme pressure to reduce the level of harm.

This chapter, while building on the findings of previous ones, attempt to offer a set of law and economics informed principles that might mitigate the identified shortcoming of the current human-centred tort law system. Namely, technical progress could occur quite quickly and thus we have to prepare our existing tort law regimes accordingly. This section offers a set of law and economics recommendations for an improved regulatory intervention which should deter AI agent's related hazards, induce optimal precaution and simultaneously preserve dynamic efficiency—incentives to innovate undistorted. Moreover, this section also addresses concerns on whether strict liability or the risk management approach (obligatory insurance or a special compensation fund) should be applied in instances where a super-intelligent AI agent causes harm. This chapter briefly explores also historical responses of legal systems to the introduction of novel technologies and suggests that law could be seen as an anti-fragile institution.

Furthermore, as argued in Chapter 5, under current rules super-intelligent AI agent might not be held liable per se for actors or omissions that cause damage, since it may not be possible to identify the party responsible for providing compensation and to require that party to make good the damage it has caused (failure of the fundamental principles of agency, causality, and foreseeability of harm). In addition, current Directive 85/374/EEC covers merely damage caused by AI agent's manufacturing defects and on condition that the injured person is able to prove the actual damage, the defect in the product and the causal relationship between damage and defect therefore strict liability or liability without fault may not be sufficient. Directive also contains a number of defences (i.e. the non-existence of technical and scientific knowledge) and safe havens (non-existence of a defect at the time of production). the technical features of the autonomous AI analytically imply that this autonomous AI and related liability discussion should be seen as a severe judgement-proof problem (addressed in previous sections). As have been previously shown the law and economics concept of judgement-proof problem informs that if injurers lack assets sufficient to pay for the losses their incentives to reduce risk will be inadequate (Shavell 1986). We argue that the judgement-proof characteristics of autonomous AI might actually completely undermine the deterrence and insurance goals of tort law.

Namely, as emphasized in Chapter 4, the evolution of a superhuman, super-intelligent AI and its capacity to develop characteristics and even personhood (and consequently also completely unexpected harmful consequences) never envisaged by its designer or producer undermines the effectiveness of the classical strict liability and other tort law instruments. Deterrence goal is corrupted irrespective of the liability rule since the judgement-proof robots (possessing autonomous AI) will not internalize costs of the accident that they might cause. Moreover, judgement-proof characteristic of the autonomous AI also implies that AI's activity levels will tend to be socially excessive and they will contribute to the excessive risk taking of the superhuman AI (Shavell 2004; Pitchford 1998; Ringleb and Wiggins 1990). Hence, as law and economics suggests tortious liability (of any kind) will not furnish adequate incentives to alleviate the risk (also there will not be any incentives for AI to purchase insurance). In other words, the insurance goal will be undermined to the extent that the judgement-proof tortfeasor (super-intelligent AI agent) will not be able to compensate fully its victims. Moreover, as shown by Logue the first-party insurance markets will also not provide an adequate response/remedy (Logue 1994).

2 How to Deal with Judgement-Proof Super-Intelligent AI Agents

The previous discussion on technical humanlike-self-awareness-self-learning features of the super-intelligent AI agent and the extrapolation of the main findings of the law and economics literature suggests that lawmakers are facing an unprecedented challenge of how to simultaneously regulate potential harmful and hazardous activity and also not to deter the innovation in the AI field. As emphasized, the judgement-proof characteristic of the super-intelligent AI agent also implies that AI's activity levels will tend to be socially excessive and they will contribute to the excessive risk taking of the autonomous AI (Shavell 2004; Pitchford 1998; Ringleb and Wiggins 1990). If AI agents will not have any assets then they will actually have no liability-related incentive to reduce risk (Shavell 1986). Their incentives to reduce the risk and harm will be completely diluted. Hence, as law and economics suggests tortious liability (of any kind) will not furnish adequate incentives to alleviate the risk (also there will not be any incentives for AI to purchase insurance). In other words, the insurance goal will be undermined to the extent that the judgement-proof tortfeasor (super-intelligent AI of any kind) will not be able to compensate fully its victims. AI agents' activity levels will tend to be socially excessive and they will contribute too much risk. Moreover, as shown by Logue the first-party insurance markets will also not provide an adequate response/remedy (Logue 1994). The triggering question then is how to mitigate the judgement-proof characteristics of a super-intelligent AI agent?

Law and economics literature does offer several potential types of policy responses to mitigate the identified potential judgement-proof characteristics of superhuman AI agent, to address the problem of dilution of liability-related incentives and its continuing, unpredictable change (self-learning and independent development) once it has left the production line and potential resulting hazards.

The first instrument is a vicarious liability (Sykes 1984; Kraakman 2000). Vicarious liability is the imposition of liability on a party related to the actual author of harm, where the vicariously liable party usually has some control over the party who directly causes harm (Shavell 2007). Classic legal forms of vicarious liability vary widely and include parents liable for harms caused by their children, contractors for harms caused by subcontractors, firms for the harms caused by employees, and lenders for the harms caused by their borrowers. Giliker (2010) in her excellent comparative treatise on vicarious liability suggests that vicarious liability lies at the heart of all common lay system of tort law. It represents not a tort, but a rule of responsibility which renders the defendant liable for the torts committed by another (Giliker 2010; Beever 2007). The classic example in English law is that of employer and employee where the employer is rendered strictly liable for the torts of his employees, provided that they are committed in the course of the tortfeasor's employment (Giliker 2010). However, one should note that under English law only the relationship of employment is capable of giving rise to vicarious liability (*Mahmud v BCCI*, 1998, AC 20). The English doctrine of vicarious liability is further confined to acts committed "in the course of employment" (Giliker 2010). Civil law systems on the other hand do not restrain themselves to the employment relationships and the vicarious liability concept is not confined to the employment contract. For example, Article 1242 of French Code Civil is now interpreted to impose liability for the wrongful acts of others under one's organization, management, and control (Terré et al. 2009). German law on the other hand initially refused to accept a general principle of vicarious liability and sought to retain an underlying basis of fault (Giliker 2010). However, today it recognizes strict liability for the torts of others and employs a variety of techniques to find such a liability and the emphasis on "fault" has been dismissed as an "embarrassment" and "historical mistake" (Giliker 2010). Thus, the German Civil Code (BGB) in Article 831(1) on vicarious agents carrying out tasks for another provides:

> A person who uses another person to perform task is liable to make compensation for the damage that the other unlawfully inflicts on a third party when carrying out the task. Liability in damages does not apply if the principal exercises reasonable care when selecting the person deployed and, to the extent that he is to procure devices or equipment or to manage the business activity, in the procurement or management, or if the damage would have occurred even if this care had been exercised.

Shavell (1986), for example suggests that if there is another party (principal) who has some control over the behaviour of the party whose assets are limited (agent), then the principal can be held vicariously liable for the losses caused by the agent. Classic law and economics literature offers two major reasons that vicarious liability may be socially desirable. First is that the injurer may not have proper information about the reduction of harm, whereas the vicariously liable party may have good, or at least superior, information and be able to influence the risk-reducing behaviour of the injurer (Cooter and Porat 2014; Shavell 2007; Posner 2014). The second reason is that vicarious liability may help to ameliorate the judgement-proof problem as it applies to the injurer (Shavell 1986). Under classic law and economics argument the vicariously liable party's assets are at risk as well as the injurer's, giving the vicariously liable party a motive to reduce risk or to moderate the injurer's activity level (Kraakman 2000; Schäfer and Ott 2004; Shavell 2007). Law and economics literature identifies various ways in which the vicariously liable party can affect the injurer's level of activity. For example, vicariously liable parties may be able to affect the behaviour of tortfeasors in some direct manner (e.g. employer does not allow employee to transport hazardous goods), vicariously liable parties may themselves take precaution that alter the risk that tortfeasors present (e.g. employer can purchase a safer and better truck to transport such hazardous goods) or vicariously liable parties may control participation in activities because they act as gatekeepers—they are able to prevent tortfeasors from engaging in their activity by withholding financing or a required service (Sykes 1984; Kraakman 2000; Schäfer and Ott 2004; Shavell 2007).

However, according to Shavell (2007) and Pitchford (1995) the main disadvantage of vicarious liability is that it increases litigation costs, since vicariously liable parties can be sued as well as the injurer. Moreover, Schäfer and Ott (2004) and Veljanovski (1982) argue that making employer completely liable for all damages caused by the employee would be efficient, since under incomplete and asymmetric information no liability would be an efficient solution.

Given the aforesaid, vicarious liability (indirect reduction of risk) and a specific principal–agent relationship between the owner (human, that employs super-intelligent AI agent) and her autonomous AI agent should be introduced in order to mitigate potential super-intelligent AI agent's harmful activity. One could even argue that we would have to introduce a legal institution that would slightly resemble the one of old Roman law institute between principal (*pater familias*) and his slave or child (agent). Namely, if the slave or child in Roman empire committed a tort the "paterfamilias" would be held liable to pay damages on their behalf unless he chose to hand over the culprit to the victim—the doctrine of "noxal" surrender (Borkowski and du Plessis 2005; Thomas 1976). In a sense a super-intelligent AI agent would be then in a similar situation to a roman slave or child (i.e. as an intelligent agent/slave whose acts might be ascribed to a principal, without the agent being treated as a full legal person itself; Turner 2019).

If we extrapolate the concept of vicarious liability upon the problem of potentially judgement-proof super-intelligent AI agent then the human principal (owner of the super-intelligent AI agent) should be held vicariously liable for the losses caused by his/her agent (super-intelligent AI agent). As long as the human principal can observe her super-intelligent AI agents' level of care then the imposition of vicarious liability will induce the human principal to compel the super-intelligent AI agent to exercise optimal care. In other words, extension of liability should lead indirectly to reduction of risk.

How would then such a vicarious liability be applied to super-intelligent AI agent? Turner (2019) offers an example of a police force which employs patrol AI agents which might according to such a rule be vicariously liable in instances where such a patrolling AI agent assaults an innocent person during its patrol. Moreover, unilateral or autonomous actions of super-intelligent AI agents which are not foreseeable do not necessarily operate (as in the instance of negligence or product liability—see Chapter 4) so as to break the chain of causation between the person held liable and the harm (Dam van 2007; Giliker 2010; Turner 2019).

Yet, law and economics literature identifies several additional significant shortcomings of the vicarious liability (Shavell 2004; Schäfer and Ott 2004). For example, if human principal is not able to observe and control super-intelligent AI agent's level of care (and also has no observation capacity) then she or he will generally not be able to induce AI agent's level of activity and consequently to reduce potential harm (Shavell 2004). If, on the other hand, principal can exert control over super-intelligent AI agent's level of activity than such vicarious liability will induce the principal to reduce AI's participation in a risky activity (and achieving efficient level of such activity). However, what if a super-intelligent AI agent is indeed, as suggested in Chapters 4 and 5 completely autonomous, self-learning, can develop emergent properties, and can adapt its behaviour and actions to the environment? In such circumstances the imposition of vicarious liability might be due to the principal's inability to observe and control super-intelligent AI agents' level of care completely inadequate and will fail to deter and prevent potential harm from occurring. Namely, the human principal's inability to observe and control super-intelligent AI agent's level of care will distort vicariously liable person's (human principal) motive to reduce risk or to moderate the AI agent's activity level. Furthermore, the vicarious liability is usually limited to a certain sphere of activities undertaken by the agent (Giliker 2010; Dam van 2007). This implies that not every act of a super-intelligent AI agent will necessarily be ascribable to the human principal. If the super-intelligent AI agent, while learning from its own variable experience and interacting with its environment in a unique manner, is strays further and further from its delineated tasks, the more likely is that there will be a gap in liability. As Turner (2019) suggests at some point the primary tortfeasor (AI agent) is cut loose from being the responsibility of its potential principal. In addition, if the potential principle would be for example a company (either corporation or limited liability company) that employs super-intelligent AI agents then also such a company itself might be judgement-proof due to the size of a company or amount of assets. Hence, the deterrence effect of such a vicarious liability would be undermined and will fail to provide incentives to the firms for an efficient amount of care and precaution.

In such a scenario law and economics literature suggests the introduction of the whole arsenal of economic and legal institutions that might address the aforementioned shortcomings of vicarious liability and to enable mitigation of such an extreme AI agent's judgement-proof problem and continuous change of a product. Generally speaking, the problem can be solved by some form of mandatory insurance that would correct for the inefficiency that super-intelligent AI agent's judgement-proof problem causes. Such a compulsory purchase of liability insurance coverage would require from principals a minimum level of liability insurance for having, employing, or using super-intelligent AI agents. The tortfeasor or his principal would have to pay an insurance premium that matches the expected damages (Schäfer and Ott 2004). However, as observed by Schäfer and Ott (2004) although efficiency in such cases is only guaranteed in the presence of mandatory insurance, it is often the case that "the political process either prevents the passing of legislation for mandatory insurance or sets the minimum insurance premium too low." Secondly, a legislator could introduce a principal's mandatory minimum asset requirement needed to engage in an activity. Yet, such an instrument might as Shavell (2004) suggests also exclude from the risky activities those principals of super-intelligent AI agents that would be able and willing to pay for the expected losses—even though they might be unable to pay for actual losses and harms.

Another powerful means of tackling the effects of judgement-proofness of a super-intelligent AI agent (and/or of his principal) is via a direct *ex ante* regulation of AI agent's risk-creating behaviour. That is, while liability law functions ex post or after the damage has occurred, administrative regulation functions prior to the damage occurring by setting and enforcing standards and applying sanctions in the event of violation (Schäfer and Ott 2004). Schäfer and Ott (2004) also suggest that the prescribed fines can be relatively low in comparison to the potential damages yet not too low in order to induce efficient deterrence. Thus, regulatory agencies would have to issue a detailed set of rules that would *ex ante* govern the entire behaviour, employment, functions, scope of its applicability, sectors in which AI agents may act and operating standards of super-intelligent AI agents. Shavell (2004) points out that such direct *ex ante* regulation will help to form principal's and manufacturer's incentives to *ex ante* reduce risk as a precondition for engaging in an AI-related activity. In other words, such regulation would, as Shavell (2004) suggests, force parties to "reduce risks in socially beneficial ways that would not be induced by the threat of liability, due to its dulled effect from the judgement-proof problem." However, as shown in Chapters 2 and 3 regulatory authority's ability to devise appropriate regulations might be limited by its knowledge, information asymmetries, and transaction costs.

Fourth, the employment of specific *ex ante* compulsory safety standards regulating AI agent's risk-creating behaviour (Faure and Pertain 2019; Kornhauser and Revesz 1998; Menell 1998) could be employed as an additional institutional mechanism to tackle the effects of judgement-proof super-intelligent AI. Shavell points out that such safety standards will help to form principal's and manufacturer's incentives *to ex ante* reduce risk as a precondition for engaging in an activity (Shavell 2004). Unfulfillment of such safety standards will then result in an automatic regulatory ban of AI agent's activity in a certain field or industry. However, these safety standards should be combined with compulsory *ex ante* registration of all super-intelligent AI agents and also of all principals (either human or companies) that employ such AI agents. Namely, a super-intelligent AI agent might still have excessive incentive to engage in risky activity, since such *ex ante* safety regulation does not impose on AI the expected losses caused by its activity. Karnow (1996) and Pagallo (2013) for example argue specifically that for intelligent machines we have to set up the so-called "Turing Registries." Accordingly, every intelligent AI agent would be submitted to a testing and certification process to quantify the certification based on a spectrum where the higher the intelligence and autonomy (and hence greater consequences of failure) the higher the registration fee payable to register that AI agent into the working environment (Karnow 1996; Buyers 2018). Evidently, super-intelligent AI agents would be prohibited to use worldwidely without this certification and registration.

The fifth possibility to address the problem of dilution of liability-related incentives is regulation of liability insurance coverage by implementing a strict liability insurance-based model for super-intelligent AI agents and the principals' and companies' minimum asset requirements (Buyers 2018; Shavell 2004). For example, persons or firms with assets less than some specified amount could be prevented from engaging in an AI agent-related activity. According to Shavell (2004) such an approach would ensure that parties who do engage in activity have enough at stake to be led to take adequate care. One could also by piercing the veil of incorporation design an extension of liability from actual AI tortfeasor to the company. Additional institutional mechanisms, supplementing all previously discussed, to address the problem of dilution of liability-related incentives would be the introduction of corrective taxes that would *ex ante* equal to the expected harm and the establishment of an EU or worldwide strict liability publicly-privately-financed insurance fund.

Sixth, lawmakers and our societies could actually resort to criminal liability to mitigate the principal diluted incentives. Namely, since a super-intelligent AI agent will be in line with the proposed concept (Chapter 5) judgement-proof, the criminal liability should be imposed upon the principal.

Finally, we should briefly address the question of whether the law of negligence and strict liability could address the shortcoming of vicarious liability. Namely, under the negligence rule the injurers will be led to take due care, assuming that due care equals optimal care (Shavell 2007). However, one should also recall our previous discussion in Chapters 5 and 6 showing that current human-centred law of negligence may indeed due to identified shortcomings of the current fundamental principles of foreseeability and causality (necessary law of negligence's requirements for establishing liability), fail to achieve optimal risk internalization, precaution and deterrence of opportunism. As argued in Chapter 5, under current rules super-intelligent AI agent might not be held liable per se for actors or omissions that cause damage, since it may not be possible to identify the party responsible for providing compensation and to require that party to make good the damage it has caused (failure of the fundamental principles of agency, causality, and foreseeability of harm). Namely, the key question in the law of negligence is generally whether the defendant acted in the same way as the average, reasonable person in that situation. One option suggested by Abbot (2018) would be to ask what the reasonable designer or user of the AI agent might have done in the circumstances. Yet, as already emphasized under the current law of negligence such a solution runs into difficulties in instances where there is no human operator of the AI agent on whom liability could be easily fixed (Hubbard 2015).

Moreover, an AI agent designed for a specific purpose might still cause harm through some form of unforeseeable development and as Turner (2019) suggests the "more unpredictable the manner of failure, the more difficult it will be to hold the user or designer responsible without resorting to a form of strict liability." Abbot (2018) proposed that if a manufacturer or retailer can show that an autonomous AI agent is safer than a reasonable person, then the supplier should for example be merely liable in negligence rather than strict liability for harm caused by the AI agent. Yet, such a solution applying "reasonable AI agent" standard might be again difficult and due to the judgement-proof problem suffers the same shortcomings as a vicarious liability. Moreover, the classic tort law standard of "foreseeable damage" will be corrupted by the increasingly unforeseeable AI agent's action (Karnow 2015).

Could identified shortcomings of the existing law of negligence and vicarious liability still be mitigated by for example strict or product liability (implying that the *ex ante* regulatory intervention is not warranted)? Such product liability can be for example found in the EU's Product Liability Directive of 1985 (Council Directive 85/374/EEC 25 July 1985). Under the rule of strict liability, injurers must pay for accident losses that they cause. Classic law and economics literature suggests that under such a rule injurers will theoretically (all conditions satisfied) be induced to choose both their level of care and their level of activity optimal (Jackson et al. 2003; Shavell 2007). Justifications for such a strict liability also include to ensure that the victim is properly compensated, to encourage those engaged in dangerous activities to take precaution and to place the costs of such activities on those who stand to benefit most (Faure and Pertain 2019; MacKaay 2015; Posner 2014; Shavell

2007). However, as already examined in Chapter 6, product liability regimes operate on the assumption that the product does not continue to change and self-develop in an unpredictable manner once it has left the production line. As shown throughout this book the super-intelligent AI agent does not follow this paradigm. Moreover, as Turner (2019) notes, current EU and US systems of strict liability are subject to a number of defences (safe heavens) which may prove overly permissive when applied to producers of super-intelligent AI. For example, current Product Liability Directive of 1985 (Council Directive 85/374/EEC 25 July 1985) in Article 7 contains such non-liability safe heavens and states:

> ...having regard to the circumstances, it is probable that the defect which caused the damage did not exist at the time when the product was put into circulation by him or that this defect came into being afterwards; or...that the state of scientific and technical knowledge at the time when he put the product into circulation was not such as to enable the existence of the defect to be discovered.

Obviously, such non-liability safe heavens will enable producers of super-intelligent AI agents to take advantage of such safe heavens and thereby undermining the overall effectiveness of liability-related incentive system. Thus, current EU Product Liability Directive of 1985 (Council Directive 85/374/EEC 25 July 1985) will have to be reformed if its scope is to extend to super-intelligent AI agents in an effective and predictable manner. For example, lawmakers could consider introducing AI manufacturer's strict liability which should be supplemented with a requirement that an unexcused violation of statutory safety standard is negligence per se. Moreover, the compliance with regulatory standard could not relieve the injurer's principal from a tort liability. Thus, per se rule (violation of regulatory standard implies tort liability—also for strict liability) should be applied also for AI related torts and the compliance defence of an AI manufacturer or its principal should not be recognized as an excuse. Yet, such amendments are still not able to address the essence of the problem implying that product liability regime operates on the assumption that the product does not continue to change in an unpredictable manner once it has left the production line. If one than employs "let the machine learn" concept the argument that a designer should have foreseen the risk becomes harder to sustain. Yet, as shown in Chapter 4 the new super-intelligent AI generation will autonomously learn from their own variable experience and interact with their environment in a unique and unforeseeable manner. Thus, product liability alone will not suffice to *ex ante* address the potential AI-related hazards and harms.

Having said all that, the informed lawmaker should combine strict liability with vicarious liability—strict liability of manufacturer and vicarious liability of principal (principal either legal or physical person). Yet, since product liability regime operates on the assumption that the product does not continue to change in an unpredictable manner once it has left the production line, such a combination might not be adequate. Furthermore, also the producers of super-intelligent AI agents themselves might be judgement-proof due to their size. The classic debate on the two different means of controlling hazardous activities, namely *ex post* liability for harm done and *ex ante* safety regulation may, due to identified shortcomings and judgement-proofness of a super-intelligent AI agent, boil down to question of efficient regulatory timing and *ex ante* regulation. The problem is that if you have standing but you cannot "represent" yourself, society is effectively back to regulation. Namely, identified shortcomings of tort law system in dealing with AI related hazards could be seen as a form of a market failure (judgement-proof problem is actually problem of prohibitively high transaction costs and information asymmetries) which is accompanied by private law failure.

As suggested in Chapter 3 such combination represents the prima facie case for regulatory intervention and as a rule of thumb, regulatory intervention is warranted if, and only if the costs of such intervention do not exceed its benefits. Obviously, previously discussed AI's potential to cause unprecedented hazards and harms (Chapters 4 and 5) satisfies proposed rule of thumb and warrants *ex ante* regulatory intervention. Such a specific worldwide *ex ante* regulatory intervention should, in order to address the identified shortcomings of liability-related tort law system, encompass at least the following: (a) mandatory insurance addressing inefficiencies caused by super-intelligent AI agent's judgement-proof problem (e.g. mandatory purchase of liability insurance coverage would require from principals a minimum level of liability insurance for having, employing or using super-intelligent AI agents); (b) direct *ex ante* regulation of AI agent's risk-creating behaviour—operating standards (i.e. a detailed set of rules that would *ex ante* govern the entire behaviour, employment, functions, scope of its applicability, sectors in which super-intelligent AI agents may act, and substantive operating standards of super-intelligent AI agents); (c) principal's minimum asset requirement needed to engage in an activity; (d) compulsory purchase of liability insurance coverage for principal; (e) "Turing" registries for human principals and AI agents (i.e. every intelligent AI agent would be submitted to a testing and certification process to quantify the certification based on a spectrum where the higher the intelligence and autonomy the higher the registration fee payable to register that AI agent into the working environment); (e) principal's criminal liability; (f) extension of liability from actual injurer (AI agent) to the company—piercing the veil of incorporation; (g) corrective taxes equal to expected harm; (h) criminal liability of principals, AI producers, and designers; and (i) establishment of publicly-privately-financed insurance fund.

3 Special Electronic Legal Personality

Could the previously discussed judgement-proof problem be ameliorated by awarding to the super-intelligent AI agent a specific legal status and making it the owner of assets? Regarding the specific legal status of AI agents EU Parliament in its Resolution on Civil Law Rules in Robotics (P8_TA (2017) 0051) in paragraph 59 recommends:

> creating a specific legal status for robots in the long run, so that at least the most sophisticated autonomous robots could be established as having the status of electronic persons responsible for making good any damage they may cause.

Perhaps this was indeed a public relations stunt but in its original wording EU Parliament suggested that EU should create a specific legal status for robots so that at least the most sophisticated autonomous robots could be established as having the status of electronic persons responsible for making good any damage they may cause, and possibly applying electronic personality to cases where robots (AI agents) make autonomous decisions or otherwise interact with third parties independently. Moreover, also Solum (1992), Wright (2001), Teubner (2007), and Koops et al. (2010) argue that legal personality should be granted to AI and that there is no compelling reason to restrict the attribution of action exclusively to humans and social systems. Moreover, Allen and Widdison (1996) suggest that when an AI is capable of developing its own strategy, it should make sense that the AI is held responsible for its independent actions. Are such a suggestion supported by the law and economics insights?

Obviously, an establishment of a special electronic person for a super-intelligent AI agent that would have its own legal personality and responsibility for potential damages should be from the law and economics perspective catastrophic. Namely, under such a proposal the AI agent itself would be legally responsible for damage, rather than the owner or manufacturer. This would then also imply that AI agents will own financial assets and be subject to sanctions if they do not comply. As this book shows in the Chapter 6 this at best does not make any sense and at worst might have disastrous consequences. Namely, as shown in Chapter 6 if we would imprison or sanction robot for non-payment or for causing harm, why would it care at all. Identified judgement-proof problem will dilute AI agent's incentives to reduce risk which materializes due to its complete indifference to the *ex ante* possibility of being found liable by the legal system for harms done to others and complete indifference to the potential accident liability (the value of expected sanction equals zero). This problem of dilution of incentives (broad judgement-proof definition) is as, we argue in Chapter 6, distinct from the problem that scholars and practitioners usually perceive as a "judgement-proof problem" which is generally identified with injurer's inability to pay fully for losses and victims' inability to obtain complete compensation (Huberman et al. 1983; Keeton and Kwerel 1984).

Thus, the employed broad definition of a judgement-proof problem encompasses all potential sources of dilution of incentives to reduce risk and not merely the narrow tortfeasor's inability to pay for the damages. Consequently, recognizing a legal personality to a super-intelligent AI agent might open the Pandora box of moral hazard and opportunism (on the sides of human principals, users, and owners) and will exacerbate the judgement-proof problem of a super-intelligent AI agent. However, one might consider a specific principal–agent legal relationship between the principal (human, that employs AI agents) and her super-intelligent AI agent.

4 Tinbergen Golden Rule of Thumb and Optimal Regulatory Timing

In the previous two sections we discussed the judgement-proofness of super-intelligent AI agents, related dilution of liability-related incentives making such AI agents de facto immune from the existing incentive stream of the human-centred tort law system. As we emphasized the classic debate on the two different means of controlling hazardous activities, namely *ex post* liability for harm done and *ex ante* safety regulation then boils down to the question of efficient regulatory timing and *ex ante* regulation. In Chapter 3 we examined the main principles of efficient regulatory intervention and as a rule of thumb suggested that regulatory intervention is warranted if, and only if the costs of such intervention do not exceed its benefits. Recall that the argument for such a rule of thumb is that either regulatory solution may be no more successful in correcting the inefficiencies than the market or private law, or that any efficiency gains to which it does give rise may be outweighed by increased transaction costs or misallocations created in other sectors of economy. Since regulatory intervention is justified, the next two questions that trigger our attention are how should we solve the regulatory problem of theoretical indeterminacy and what would be the optimal regulatory timing. In other words, how many regulatory instruments do we need and whether we should act immediately or wait until the super-intelligent AI agents become reality?

The forms question theoretical indeterminacy is a major problem because it makes it impossible to derive policy recommendations and full explanations from law and economics theories (De Geest 2012). Law and economics has become one of the leading research programs in law. Yet, after four decades it still cannot answer simple questions such as what is for example the optimal tortious liability regime related to precaution and deterrence. Theoretical indeterminacy is a major problem because it makes it impossible to derive policy recommendations and full explanations from law and economics theories (De Geest 2012). De Geest (2012) shows that most of the indeterminacy is caused by trying to solve many problems with a single legal instrument. Doing so is problematic for two reasons. First, such a single rule will be a compromise rule, which is not very effective at solving all the problems. Second, choosing the right compromise requires information on the relative social importance of all the problems; such information is nearly impossible to get, and therefore makes the discussion indeterminate. The solution De Geest (2012) proposes is simple: employ a separate rule or doctrine per problem.

Hence, effective lawmaker should, while tackling the inequality problem, design its policy in line with the golden Tinbergen rule—*N* problems requires *N* solutions. This rule, employed in natural sciences as a general research maxim, was formulated by the Dutch economics Nobel laureate, Jan Tinbergen in 1952 and is generally stated as "for each policy objective, at least one policy instrument is needed - there should be at least the same number of instruments as there are targets" (Tinbergen 1952). Hence, an informed lawmaker should identify multiple sources/causes of hazards and inefficiencies that super-intelligent AI agents may cause and for each of them design its own *ex ante* regulatory instrument. Legal rules should be designed to *ex ante* deter/prevent materialization of hazards and harms that are caused by judgement-proofness of super-intelligent AI agents. Potential set of all different rules have been offered in previous two sections and this golden Tinbergen rule of thumb also implies that all these regulatory instruments should be used simultaneously to address multiple sources of harm and hazards.

The second issue relates to the regulatory dilemma of whether to act, regulate now, or rather employ "wait and see what happens" strategy. Encompassing previous law and economics suggestions regulatory intervention addressing the judgement-proofness of super-intelligent AI agents should be in line with the worst-case scenario principle enacted now (*ex ante*). Namely, the new super-intelligent AI agents might cause unforeseeable fatal losses and due to the identified shortcomings of the *ex post* mechanisms the *ex ante* regulatory intervention is deemed necessary. Lawmakers should not employ the so-called "let's wait and see what happens" strategy but should prepare (regulate) *ex ante* for the probability of the so-called "worst-case scenario" where AI will be, as Russell (2019) suggests, the last event in human history. The regulatory-designing timing is, as this book attempts to show, essential. Lawmakers should not wait and see, since consequences may indeed be ruinous, but rather legislate now.

In a groundbreaking paper, Gersen and Posner (2007) investigated the optimal timing of legislative action and point out that decisions about the timing of legal intervention are often as important as decisions about the content of new law. They argue that lawmakers cannot know with certainty what the appropriate law will be in the future and that therefore cannot know with certainty what the future stream of benefits from the law will be (Gersen and Posner 2007). In addition, the costs of implementing the new law are largely sunk and irreversible (e.g. outlay of resources in formulating and enforcing the law) where the costs of implementing the new law cannot be recovered if the law turns out to be inappropriate. Timing of the investment becomes a critical issue for such irreversible investments (Gersen and Posner 2007; Luppi and Parisi 2009). In economic terms the lawmaker's decision to invest in the new law represents "opportunity costs" of giving up the option to implement the law in the future.

However, there is also an "opportunity benefit" in investing today. Parisi and Ghei (2007) offer a formal model where three attributes that lawmaking shares with investment are identified: (a) the costs of lawmaking can typically not be recovered if the rule proves to be ineffective or undesirable at a later point in time; (b) the future benefits of legislation are uncertain; and (c) lawmakers have the option to postpone the change in the current legal rules. The literature also offers the conception of optimal time to legislate, according to which a benevolent and rational lawmaker should enact a new rule (or modify an existing one) when the present value of the expected benefits from the legal innovation are at least as large as its costs (Pindyck 1991; Parisi and Ghei 2007). Obviously, the optimal timing of lawmaking is affected by the presence of uncertainty, since after the uncertainty materializes the desirability of the law changes accordingly. Gersen and Posner (2007) investigate several potential timing rules and emphasize the significance of the so-called "anticipatory legislation" rule. They suggest that under this option the law is enacted at time $t = 1$ (imposing certain enactment costs k), to take effect in period $t = 2$ and such timing allows the lawmaker to repeal the statue if information obtained in the first period show that the enactment is inefficient (Gersen and Posner 2007). Thus, the law will become effective only if the effects of the law are positive and such timing rule offers an option of exit through repeal. Such an anticipatory legislation has an advantage in comparison with immediate legislation or deferred legislation since the legislative costs are incurred at period $t = 1$ than in period $t = 2$ where such costs might be much higher (Gersen and Posner 2007).

Moreover, such anticipatory legislation has lower adjustment costs since stakeholders can more confidently rely on the public good being created—i.e. such legislation increases the probability that the public good will be created (Gersen and Posner 2007). The optimal timing of the legal intervention is thus crucial, since delays in lawmaking decisions may come at a cost. The exponent rise of the AI technology over time is increasing the costs of lawmaking and such costs in future may be, taking into account the precautionary principle, even higher. Thus, current lawmaking initiatives and activities employ the "anticipatory legislation" approach, which is due to the specific features of the AI in line with the theory on the optimal timing of legal intervention.

5 Liability for Harm Versus Safety Regulation

In his seminal paper on liability for harm versus regulation of safety professor Shavell paved the way towards an analytical understanding of the optimal employment of tort liability and/or regulatory standards. Shavell instrumentally addressed the effects of liability rules and direct regulation upon the rational self-interested party's decision-making process (Shavell 1984). Namely, liability in tort and the safety regulation represent two different approaches for controlling activities that create risks of harm and that induce the optimal amount of precaution. Tort liability is private in nature and works not by social command but rather indirectly, through the deterrent effect of damage actions that may be brought once harm occurs, whereas standards and ex ante regulations are public in character and modify behaviour in an immediate way through requirements that are imposed before the actual occurrence of harm (Shavell 1984). However, as Shavell (1984) emphasizes there have been major mistakes made in the use of liability and safety regulation. Regulation, when applied exclusively, had often, due to manifold problems, proved to be inadequate, whereas also tort liability might provide, due to causation problems, suboptimal deterrence incentives (Shavell 1984; Epstein 1982). Shavell (1984) also argues that regulatory fines are identical to tortious liability in that they create incentives to reduce risks by making parties pay for the harm they cause. Yet fines also suffer from the inability to pay for harm and from the possibility that violators would escape public agency (Shavell 1984). Nevertheless, as Shavell (1984) emphasizes, regulatory fines have an advantage in instances where private suits (and related tortious liability) would not be brought due to difficulty in establishing causation or where harms are widely dispersed.

In addition, Rose-Ackerman (1991b) suggests that regulation (statues) should generally dominate so long as agencies can employ rule-making to shape policy. The tort rules should consequently be limited to areas of activity not covered by regulation and to situations in which courts can complement the regulatory (statutory) scheme with a supplementary enforcement and compensation mechanism. Whereas Schmitz (2000) argues that the joint use of liability and safety regulation is optimal if wealth varies among injurers.

This book also suggests that *ex ante* regulation and *ex post* liability-related tort law regime should be applied simultaneously (not if/or but and). *Ex post* liability and *ex ante* regulation (safety standards) are generally viewed as substitutes for correcting externalities, and the usual recommendation is to employ the policy which leads to lower administrative costs. However, Schmitz (2000) shows that joint use of liability and regulation can enhance social wealth. Namely, regulation removes problems affecting liability, while liability limits the cost of regulation (Rose-Ackerman 1991a, b). General regulatory standards should be settled at a lower level of care (lower than optimal) and combined with tort law instruments (De Geest and Dari-Mattiachi 2005). Namely, by introducing an *ex ante* regulatory standard, the principal and his super-intelligent AI agent might be prevented from taking low levels of precaution and might find convenient with the regulatory standard despite the judgement-proof problem.

6 Regulatory Sandboxes

The judgement-proofness of super-intelligent AI agents is a reoccurring theme of our examination. The *ex ante* regulatory intervention to mitigate identified inefficiencies appears as urgent. However, the triggering question if how we would know which of the regulatory tools that are at our disposal are effective and really work in practice and which hinders innovation ad progress? This question of practical effectiveness could be examined in the so-called "regulatory sandboxes." A regulatory sandbox is a process and a tool for regulation. It is described as a "laboratory environment" but its key function is to test innovations against the existing regulatory framework (Allen 2019a). This function is achieved via a process involving the participating business entities and the regulator (Allen 2019a; Zetzsche et al. 2017–2018).

Similarly to its namesake, "regulatory sandboxes" aim to mitigate a risk. Yet, the nature of the risk is substantively different compared to the risk in a computer system (Yordanova 2019). This requires a different and, more importantly, adaptive approach in constructing different sandboxes, even in relation to the different participants in each of them. Moreover, the regulatory sandbox is a legal fiction and, as such, it is subject to the rules of legal logic (Yordanova 2019). For example, Ringe and Ruof (2020) propose a regulatory "sandbox"—an experimentation space—as a step towards a regulatory environment where new AI technologies and businesses can thrive. A sandbox would according to Ringe and Ruof (2020) allow market participants to test super-intelligent AI agent's advice services in the real market, with real consumers, but under close scrutiny of the supervisor. Ringe and Ruof (2020) also argue that the benefit of such an approach is that it fuels the development of new business practices and reduces the "time to market" cycle of financial innovation while simultaneously safeguarding consumer protection. At the same time, a sandbox allows for mutual learning in a field concerning a little-known phenomenon, both for firms and for the regulator (Ringe and Ruof 2020). This would, as Ringe and Ruof (2020) suggest, help reducing the prevalent regulatory uncertainty for all market participants. They also propose a "guided sandbox," operated by the EU Member States, but with endorsement, support, and monitoring by EU institutions (Ringe and Ruof 2020). This innovative approach would be somewhat unchartered territory for the EU, and thereby also contribute to the future development of EU financial market governance as a whole (Ringe and Ruof 2020).

Obviously, Ringe and Ruof (2020) offer an optimistic view on the applicability of "regulatory sandboxes" where all of our concerns on the failure of liability-related tort rules could be tested in a controlled environment and hence all AI-related concerns could be refuted. However, several other scholars and performed empirical analysis are much more sceptical and raise a number of concerns. For example, sandbox report, providing a bespoke sandbox environment for testing does not, in itself, address all the challenges a firm may face in successfully testing their innovation (FCA 2017; Allen 2019a). Based on the acquired experience in the field of FinTech and keeping in mind the EU's ambitions for a regulatory sandbox on AI, some issues are to be highlighted and need to be taken into consideration by the regulators in their future work on this matter. First, the term AI is very broad and naturally there's a clear need for careful differentiation in order for the sandbox to be functional (FCA 2017). Second, the regulatory sandbox needs transparency which must be balanced with classified and commercially sensitive information and trade secrets (FCA 2017). Thirdly, the limited number of participants may be insufficient to satisfy the market's needs and could raise some competition concerns (Yordanova 2019). Furthermore, it is not clear how a national regulator can fully participate in a regulatory sandbox when the area of regulation falls party or entirely under for example EU's competences (FCA 2017; Yordanova 2019). Last but not least, one of the key characteristics of AI is its capability of learning, meaning an AI technology coming out of the sandbox and labelled as *compliant* can change pretty rapidly and undermine the value of the sandbox process (FCA 2017; Yordanova 2019; Allen 2019a).

Moreover, Allen (2019b) suggests that these regulatory sandboxes seek to promote AI-related innovations by rolling back some of the consumer protection and prudential regulations that would otherwise apply to the firms trialling for example their financial products and services in the sandbox. While sacrificing such protections in order to promote innovation is problematic, such sacrifice may nonetheless be justifiable if, by working with innovators in the sandbox, regulators are educated about new technologies in a way that enhances their ability to effectively promote consumer protection and financial stability in other contexts (Allen 2019b). However, the market for fintech products and services transcends national and subnational borders, and Allen (2019b) predicts that as "competition amongst countries for fintech business intensifies, the phenomena of regulatory arbitrage, race to the bottom, and coordination problems are likely to drive the regulatory sandbox model towards further deregulation, and disincentivize vital information sharing amongst financial regulators about new technologies." Allen (2019b) examines several regulatory sandboxes adopted by Arizona and the Consumer Financial Protection Bureau, as well as the proposals for transnational cooperation in the form of the Global Financial Innovation Network and identifies numerous inefficiencies. Overall, we may conclude that there is reason to be pessimistic about the trajectory of the current regulatory sandbox model; the trend suggests that consumer protection, deterrence of harms, and prevention of hazards could be sacrificed in the name of promoting innovation.

7 Liability for Harm and Incentives to Innovate

In the previous section we addressed the role of "regulatory sandboxes" as an innovative tool for ex ante correction of the potential super-intelligent AI agent related inefficiencies, while simultaneously boosting AI innovations and progress. Namely, one of the main concerns of the AI businesses is the potential negative effect of proposed regulatory intervention (e.g. strict liability, Turing registries, operating standards, compulsory insurance) upon the rate of innovation (dynamic efficiency). In other words, extremely strict regulatory environment may impede AI-related technological progress, diminish productivity, and decrease overall social wealth. Hence, one may wonder if indeed proposed regulatory measures which should (*ex ante*) deal effectively with identified judgement-proofness of super-intelligent AI agents will deter innovation and impede welfare?

The essence of product liability is the appointment of the risks inherent in the modern mass production of goods. In the last decades law and economics scholarship shifted its attention towards the potential detrimental effects of different tort law regimes and product liability on the innovative activity (Manning 1997). Over the last 40 years, the core of liability law worldwidely has traversed from simple negligence to the far more complex concept of strict product liability. This change has been triumphed by many as a victory for consumers and safer products. In theory, enhanced quality, safety, and innovation should have resulted from this liability revolution. However, scholars found that the reverse occurred (Herbig and Golden 1994; Malott 1988; McGuire 1988). They show that product liability costs in the United States have prompted some manufacturers to abandon valuable new technologies, life-saving drugs, and innovative product designs (Herbig and Golden 1994; Malott 1988; McGuire 1988).

Another stream of law and economics investigated the related issues of product liability and its detrimental effects on innovations. Namely, product liability ideally should promote efficient levels of product safety, but misdirected liability efforts, various litigation mechanisms may actually depress beneficial innovations. For example, the American Medical Association and Pharmaceutical Manufacturers Association in its report from 2000 argues that innovative products are not being developed or are being withheld from the American market because of liability concerns or inability to obtain adequate insurance. Viscusi and Moore (1993) in their seminal article examined these competing effects of liability costs on product R & D intensity and new product introductions by manufacturing firms. They convincingly show that at low to moderate levels of expected liability costs, there is a positive effect of liability costs on product innovation (Viscusi and Moore 1993). Whereas, at very high levels of liability costs, the effect is negative. Moreover, they show that at the sample mean, liability costs increase R & D intensity by 15% (Viscusi and Moore 1993). The greater linkage of these effects to product R & D rather than process R & D is consistent with the increased prominence of the design defect doctrine (Viscusi and Moore 1993).

However, Kovac et al. (2020) in their recent study on the interrelationships between propensity to patent, innovative activity, and litigation and liability costs generated by different legal systems show that product liability and related litigation costs across firms and countries do not account for the failure of pharmaceutical firms to innovate. The results actually reveal that higher litigation and liability costs across firms, combined with damage caps, reversed causality, limited class actions and broad statutory excuses, between and within countries have a positive effect on the validation rate, application rate and on the stock of EPO patents (Kovac et al. 2020). Thus, proposed regulatory measures dealing effectively with identified judgement-proofness of super-intelligent AI agents are not an impediment to technological innovation but should instead be perceived as a filter that screens hazardous innovation in the AI field and provides incentive for an efficient, productive, and safe innovations and simultaneously also deter opportunism and moral hazard.

8 Historical Legal Responses to Technical Innovations: Anti-fragile Law

Discussing super-intelligent AI agents one may wonder whether humanity have faced similar technological challenges before? Could existing legal structures provide sufficient degree of anti-fragility to implement proposed regulatory measures and to deal effectively with the judgement-proof super-intelligent AI agent? If indeed "*Historia est Magistra Vitae*" (Cicero 1860) then one may indeed wonder what can history teach us?

Two thousand years ago old Roman jurists faced a pretty similar challenge and legal conundrum as super-intelligent, superhuman AI presents for current policymakers. The expansion of empire and unprecedented economic growth with the employment of slaves as a driving force of the economy actually required an invention of a unique legal institution to deal with the liability-related problems. Namely, slaves as principal's agents during their daily activities from time to time inflicted harm upon other free citizens of Rome. As economy grew and as more and more slaves have been employed into the daily economic activity (enabling exponential economic growth of Roman empire) the question arose on how to mitigate, deter these harms, and on how to allocate liability in order to deter such hazards and harms. Old Roman jurists responded ingeniously and provided a novel legal institution dealing with the judgement-proof autonomous slaves—the master–slave relationship. Insightfully, in classic roman law a "*naturalis obligatio* could result from the dealings of a slave with other persons than his master; but the master was not at all affected by such dealings" (Smith and Anthon 1858). As Smith and Anthon (1858) report, "master was only bound by the acts and dealing of the slave, when the slave was employed as his agent or instrument, in which case the master might be liable to an *Actio Exercitoria* or *Institoria*" (Gaius, IV.71). Moreover, there was "an *actio* (vicarious liability) against the master, when the slave acted by his orders" [Jussu, Quod, &c.] (Smith and Anthon 1858). Smith and Anthon also suggest that "if a slave traded with his *peculium* with the knowledge of the *dominus* or father, the *peculium* and all that was produced by it were divisible among the creditors and master in due proportions (*pro rata portione*), and if any of the creditors complained of getting less than his share, he had a *tributoria actio* against the master, to whom the law gave the power of distribution among the creditors" (Gaius, IV.72, &c.; Smith and Anthon 1858).

Thus, the idea of liability for the torts of others may be traced back to Roman law. Although Roman lawyers did not consider the liability problem as a whole nor reach any general statement of principle, specific examples of liability of a superior for wrongful acts of his agents may be found (Giliker 2010; Zweigert and Kötz 1998). Thus, old Roman jurists have provided the first institutional mechanism to mitigate the judgement-proof problem of their autonomous agents (slaves). However, it is questionable to what extent Roman law has, in fact influenced the modern doctrine of tortious liability (Zimmermann 2001). Yet, Ibbetson (1999) traces the common law doctrine of the liability for the torts of others back to the medieval times. The background history of modern vicarious liability is therefore, as Giliker (2010) suggests, best understood in the context of nineteenth-century codifications where economic advances demanded the growing attention to the employer–employee relationship. The rise of corporations, the impact of third industrial revolution (technological breakthroughs) in terms of accident causation rendered the question of liability interested and insured third parties more and more relevant (Giliker 2010). Such development impacted not only the growth and legal sophistication of vicarious liability, but also on its role and significance in the law of tort (Giliker 2010).

Namely, throughout the history the introduction of every new technology in essence presented a problem to existing legal institutions and their dealing with harms and hazards caused by such a novel technology. Generally, legal systems responded with previously discussed standards (see Chapter 5) of foreseeability and reasonableness. Consider for example the *Guille v. Swan* case (Supreme Court of New York, 19 Johns. 381, 1822) where Guille ascended in a balloon in the vicinity of Swan's garden, and descended into his garden. When he descended his body was hanging out of the car of the balloon in a very perilous situation, and he called to a person at work in Swan's field, to help him, in a voice audible to the pursuing crowd. After the balloon descended, it dragged along over potatoes and radishes, about thirty feet, when Guille was taken out. The balloon was carried to a barn at the farther end of the premises. When the balloon descended, more than two hundred persons broke into Swan's garden through the fences, and came on his premises; beating down his vegetables and flowers. The damage done by Guille, with his balloon, was about $15, but the crowd did much more. The plaintiff's damages, in all, amounted to $90 (*Guille v. Swan* case, Supreme Court of New York, 19 Johns. 381, 1822). The Court stated:

> The intent with which an act is done, is by no means the test of the liability of a party to an action of trespass. If the act cause the immediate injury, whether it was intentional, or unintentional, trespass is the proper action to redress the wrong.... In *Leame v Bray* (3 East Rep 595) Lord Ellenborough said: If I put in motion a dangerous thing, as if I let loose a dangerous animal, and leave to hazard what may happen and mischief ensue, I am answerable in trespass; and if one (he says) put an animal or carriage in motion, which causes an immediate injury to another, he is the actor, the causa causans....Where an immediate act is done by the co-operation, or the joint act of several persons, they are all trespassers, and may be sued jointly or severally; and any one of them is liable for the injury done by all. To render one man liable in trespass for the acts of others, it must appear, either that they acted in concert, or that the act of the individual sought to be charged, ordinarily and naturally, produced the

> acts of the others. I will not say that ascending in a balloon is an unlawful act, for it is not so; but it is certain that the aeronaut has no control over its motion horizontally; he is at the sport of the winds, and is to descend when and how he can; his reaching the earth is a matter of hazard. He did descend on the premises of the plaintiff below, at a short distance from the place where he ascended. Now, if his descent, under such circumstances, would, ordinarily and naturally, draw a crowd of people about him, either from curiosity, or for the purpose of rescuing him from a perilous situation; all this he ought to have foreseen, and must be responsible for. Whether the crowd heard him call for help or not, is immaterial; he had put himself in a situation to invite help, and they rushed forward, impelled, perhaps, by the double motive of rendering aid, and gratifying a curiosity which he had excited. ... we must consider the situation in which he placed himself, voluntarily and designedly, as equivalent to a direct request to the crowd to follow him. (*Guille v. Swan* case, Supreme Court of New York, 19 Johns. 381, 1822)

These anecdotal cases show that old rules, while dealing with the unprecedented new technologies, and when there is no legitimate use (e.g. ballooning over Manhattan or having a reservoir in very wet England) generally employed strict liability (e.g. Rylands v. Fletcher (1868) LR 3 HL 330). Obviously, the law could be perceived as an anti-fragile system that benefits from shocks and thrives when exposed to volatility, randomness, risk, and uncertainty (Taleb 2012). Taken into account the historical narrative and gradual development of ever more legally sophisticated doctrine of vicarious liability one may indeed argue that old laws and established legal mechanisms fairly addressed responsibility for harm caused by new technologies. Thus, one may indeed hypothesize that current law and regulatory tools can already offer sophisticated mechanisms that could be immediately employed (*ex ante* approach) to deter and prevent materialization of harms and hazards caused by judgement-proof super-intelligent AI agents. The bigger question is whether society's (efficiency) aims would be served better reformulating our relationship with judgement-proof super-intelligent AI agent in a more radical fashion (as proposed in this book) and whether current rules indeed cover the entire scope of super-intelligent AI.

In other words, one may wonder whether old rules are adequate or further sophistication of such rules is urgently needed. Are we able to provide them? Recall that the tort liability can be strict or negligence-based (Dari-Mattiachi and De Geest 2005). If it is strict courts have to check whether there is harm and who caused it. In case that we employ the law of negligence court must additionally check also whether tortfeasor was at fault. The last demand more work and sophistication. Not surprisingly, as we have already shown, old legal systems employed strict liability whereas current ones employ a whole plethora of different tort rules.

Why is the development of sophisticated tort law late, slow, and unequal between different jurisdictions? An economic explanation is that adjudication of strict liability is cheap whereas adjudication of negligence is labour-intensive, as proving the parties' intentions, foreseeability and causality is intrinsically difficult. In other words, as De Geest (2018) argues that sophisticated tort law is an expensive law where costs of adjudicating and enforcing of such a rule tend to be high. Namely, when the legal system's capacity is limited, it can address only the most harmful acts and as capacity grows, it can address acts that are less harmful at the margin. De Geest (2018) suggests that "older legal systems had lower capacity. They had fewer judges, attorneys, police officers and prison guards. Therefore the rules were so chosen that they required less work for the legal system. This mean faster procedures, simpler rules, and less tailor-made solutions. Unfortunately, it also meant more mistakes, and more forms of socially undesirable behaviour tolerated."

However, as the economy grows also the capacity of the legal system grows. This increased capacity than allows courts and lawmakers to employ, articulate and design rules that achieve higher-quality outcome (courts are more likely to address injustice and to discover the truth) but require more work for the courts (De Geest 2018). Therefore, in past the rules were so chosen that they required less work for the legal system. This also meant simpler rules, less tailor-made solutions but also more mistakes and more socially undesirable behaviour tolerated (De Geest 2018). Yet, since western societies have in recent decades witnessed an unprecedent economic growth and increase of wealth (North and Thomas 1973; North 1981; Kovac and Spruk 2016), legal systems started to address also very specific and complicated legal problems. Legal doctrine, scholarship, and jurisprudence became more and more perfect, devoting more and more expertise also to marginal cases of undesirable behaviour and the legal profession today is able to provide a set of advanced regulatory tools drafted exclusively to deal with the judgement-proofness of super-intelligent AI agents. As already emphasized, the bigger question is whether society is willing to reformulate our relationship with a judgement-proof super-intelligent AI agent in a more radical fashion.

9 Current Trends in Legislative Activity

Commentators argue that government AI policies generally fall into at least one of the following three categories: promoting the growth of a local AI industry; ethics and regulation for AI; and managing the problem of unemployment caused by AI (Turner 2019). Provided brief survey bellow is not intended to be a comprehensive examination of all regulatory activities since matters are developing fast and such overview will soon go out of date. Instead, this section offers some general regulatory approaches and activities.

On the EU level, the EU Parliament has in 2017 urged the EU Commission to produce a legislative proposal containing a set of detailed civil law rules on robotics and artificial intelligence (2015/2103(INL), P8_TA (2017) 0051). This proposal also includes a set of precise recommendations and also very broad proposals to the EU Commission on civil law rules on robotics. These should address such issues as liability for damages caused by a robot, produce an ethical code of conduct and also to establish a European agency for robotics and artificial intelligence. Legally speaking, this resolution is based on Article 225 TFEU and on the Council Directive 85/374/EEC which actually leaves the EU Commission with two choices, one is to produce a proposal and second is to argue why it will not follow it.

EU Parliament, while noting that the traditional rules will not suffice, emphasizes that the development of cognitive features is turning autonomous AI into agents and hence the legal responsibility arising through an AI's harmful action became a crucial issue. EU Parliament notices that the shortcoming of current legal framework are apparent in the area of contractual liability and that in relation to non-contractual liability, Directive 85/374/EEC can cover only damage caused by an AI's manufacturing defects and on condition that the injured person is able to prove the actual damage, the defect in the product and the causal relationship between damage and defect therefore strict liability or liability without the fault framework may not be sufficient. European Parliament emphasizes that draft legislation is urgently needed to clarify liability issues, especially for self-driving cars. EU Parliament also calls for a mandatory insurance scheme and a supplementary fund to ensure that victims of accidents involving driverless cars are fully compensated. Moreover, it asks the EU Commission to consider creating a specific legal status for robots in the long run, in order to establish who is liable if they cause damage. Furthermore, EU Parliament also requested the EU Commission to submit on the basis of Article 114 TFEU, a proposal for a Directive on civil law rules and to consider the designation of a European Agency for Robotics and Artificial Intelligence in order to provide the technical, ethical, and regulatory expertise. In addition, EU Parliament wonders whether: (a) strict liability or (b) the risk management approach, (c) obligatory insurance, or (d) a special compensation fund should be applied in instances where artificial intelligence causes damage. In addition, EU Parliament also wonders whether AI should be characterized in the existing legal categories or whether a new category with specific rules should be created and if the answer is affirmative then what kind of a category?

Regarding the specific legal status EU Parliament in its Resolution on Civil Law Rules in Robotics (P8_TA (2017) 0051) in paragraph 59 actually suggests that "EU should create a specific legal status for robots, so that at least the most sophisticated autonomous robots could be established as having the status of *electronic persons* responsible for making good any damage they may cause, and possibly applying electronic personality to cases where robots (AI) make autonomous decisions or otherwise interact with third parties independently."

In addition, the resolution proposes to "introduce a system of registration for 'smart robots', that is, those which have autonomy through the use of sensors and/or interconnectivity with the environment, which have at least a minor physical support, which adapt their behaviour and actions to the environment and which cannot be defined as having 'life' in the biological sense (P8_TA (2017) 0051)." The system of registration of advanced robots would be managed by a completely newly established "EU agency for robotics and artificial intelligence." This agency would also provide technical, ethical, and regulatory expertise on robotics. Conclusively, EU Parliament also proposes (a) Code of ethical conduct for robotics engineers; (b) Code for research ethics committees; (c) a licence for designers; and (d) a licence for users. EU Commission in its Communication from the Commission to the European Parliament on artificial intelligence for Europe (COM (2018) 237 final) informs that a thorough evaluation of the Product Liability Directive (85/374/EEC) has been carried out and provides that "although strict liability for producers of AI is uncontested, the precise effects of new technological developments will have to be more closely analysed." EU Commission in this Communication also explicitly questions whether "a regulatory intervention on these technologies appears appropriate and necessary and whether that intervention should be developed in a horizontal or sectoral way and whether new legislation should be enacted at EU level (COM (2018) 237 final)."

In March 2018, the European Group on Ethics in Science and New Technologies published its "Statement on Artificial Intelligence, Robotics and Autonomous systems" advocating creation of an ethical and legal framework for the design, production, use, and governance of AI, robotics, and autonomous systems. In 2019 building on the work of the group of independent experts appointed in June 2018, the EU Commission launched a pilot phase to ensure that the ethical guidelines for Artificial Intelligence (AI) development and use can be implemented in practice. As of 2019 EU Commission is taking a three-step approach: setting out the key requirements for trustworthy Artificial Intelligence, launching a large-scale pilot phase for feedback from stakeholders, and working on international consensus building for human-centric AI. EU Commission also issued seven essentials for achieving trustworthy AI which should respect all applicable laws and regulations, as well as a series of requirements; specific assessment lists aim to help verify the application of each of the key requirements: (a) human agency and oversight; (b) robustness and safety; (c) privacy and data governance; (d) transparency; (e) diversity, non-discrimination, and fairness; (f) societal and environmental well-being; and (g) accountability which requires that mechanisms should be put in place to ensure responsibility and accountability for AI. However, despite this encouraging sign the EU's regulatory agenda remains at an incipient stage.

In the United States, Trump administration appears to have abandoned the topic as a major priority (Metz 2018), whereas in Japan the Advisory Board on AI and Human Society produced a report (2017) which recommended further work on issues including ethics, law, economics, education, social impacts, and R & D. Furthermore, China for example call in April 2018 to negotiate and conclude a succinct protocol to ban the use of fully autonomous weapons systems made to the UN Group of Governmental Experts on lethal autonomous weapons systems (Kania 2018). In UK there has been until 2018 no concerted effort to develop comprehensive standards governing AI (Turner 2019).

10 Conclusions

This chapter attempts to offer a set of law and economics informed principles that might mitigate the identified shortcomings of the current human-centred tort law system. Namely, technical progress could occur quite quickly and thus we have to prepare our existing tort law regimes accordingly. This section offers a set of law and economics recommendations for an optimal regulatory intervention which should deter AI agent's related hazards, induce optimal precaution and simultaneously preserve dynamic efficiency—incentives to innovate undistorted. This chapter also investigates key policy initiatives and offers a substantive analysis of the optimal regulatory intervention. It discusses the concepts of regulatory sandboxes, negligence, strict and product liability, vicarious liability, accident compensation schemes, insurance, and the tort law and economics insights of the judgement-proof problem. Moreover, it offers a critical examination of separate legal personality, robot rights and offers a set of arguments for an optimal regulatory intervention and for an optimal regulatory timing. In addition, this chapter provides economically inspired, instrumental insights for an improved liability law regime, strict liability and principal–agent relationships. To end, there is an attempt at an anti-fragile view of the law and its persistent, robust responses to uncontemplated technological shocks and related hazards.

Bibliography

Abbot, Ryan. 2018. The Reasonable Computer: Disrupting the Paradigm of Tort Liability. *The George Washington Law Review* 86 (1): 101–143.

Allen, J. Hillary. 2019a. Regulatory Sandboxes. *George Washington Law Review* 87 (3): 579–645.

Allen, J. Hillary. 2019b. Sandbox Boundaries. *Vanderbilt Journal of Entertainment & Technology Law* 22 (2): 299–321.

Allen, Tom, and Robin Widdison. 1996. Can Computers Make Contracts? *Harvard Journal of Law & Technology* 9 (1): 26–52.

Beever, Allan. 2007. *Rediscovering the Law of Negligence*. Oxford: Oxford University Press.

Borkowski, J. Andrew, and Paul du Plessis. 2005. *Textbook on Roman Law*, 3rd ed. Oxford: Oxford University Press.

Buyers, John. 2018. *Artificial Intelligence: The Practical Legal Issues*. Somerset: Law Brief Publishing.

Cicero, Marcus Tullius. 1860. *On Oratory and Orators*, trans. J.S. Watson. New York: Harper & Brothers.

Cooter, D. Robert, and Ariel Porat. 2014. *Getting Incentives Right: Improving Torts, Contracts, and Restitution*. Princeton, NJ: Princeton University Press.

Dam van, Cees. 2007. *European Tort Law*. Oxford: Oxford University Press.

Dari-Mattiachi, Giuseppe, and Gerrit De Geest. 2005. The Filtering Effect of Sharing Rules. *Journal of Legal Studies* 34 (1): 207–237.

De Geest, Gerrit. 2012. Overcoming Theoretical Indeterminacy. *SSRN Electronic Journal*. https://doi.org/10.2139/ssrn.1990804.

De Geest, Gerrit. 2018. Old Law Is Cheap Law. In *Don't Take It Seriously: Essays in Law and Economics in Honour of Roger Van den Bergh*, ed. Michael Faure, Wicher Schreuders, and Louis Visscher, 505–525. Cambridge: Intersentia.

De Geest, Gerrit, and Giuseppe Dari-Mattiachi. 2005. Soft Regulators, Tough Judges. George Mason Law & Economics Research Paper No. 03-56.

Epstein, A. Richard. 1982. The Principles of Environmental Protection: The Case of Superfund. *Cato Journal* 2: 9.

Faure, G. Michael, and Roy A. Pertain. 2019. *Environmental Law and Economics: Theory and Practice*. Cambridge: Cambridge University Press.

Financial Conduct Authority. 2017. *Regulatory Sandbox Lessons Learned Report*. London: Financial Conduct Authority.

Gersen, E. Jacob, and Eric A. Posner. 2007. Timing Rules and Legal Institutions. *Harvard Law Review* 121 (2): 543–589.

Giliker, Paula. 2010. *Vicarious Liability in Tort: A Comparative Perspective*. Cambridge: Cambridge University Press.

Herbig, A. Paul, and James E. Golden. 1994. Differences in Forecasting Behavior Between Industrial Product Firms and Consumer Product Firms. *Journal of Business & Industrial Marketing* 9 (1): 60–69.

Hubbard, F. Patrick. 2015. Sophisticated Robots: Balancing Liability, Regulation, and Innovation. *Florida Law Review* 66: 1803–1862.

Huberman, Gur, David Mayers, and Clifford W. Smith. 1983. Optimal Insurance Policy Indemnity Schedules. *Bell Journal of Economics* 14 (2): 415–426.

Ibbetson, J. David. 1999. *A Historical Introduction to the Law of Obligations*. Oxford: Oxford University Press.

Jackson, E. Howell, Louis Kaplow, Steven M. Shavell, Kip W. Viscusi, and David Cope. 2003. *Analytical Methods for Lawyers*. New York: Foundation Press.

Kania, Elsa. 2018. China's Strategic Ambiguity and Shifting Approach to Lethal Autonomous Weapons Systems. Lawfare Blog.

Karnow, E.A. Curtis. 1996. Liability for Distributed Artificial Intelligence. *Berkeley Technology Law Journal* 11 (1): 147–183.

Karnow, E.A. Curtis. 2015. The Application of Traditional Tort Theory to Embodied Machine Intelligence. In *Robot Law*, ed. Ryan Calo, Michael Froomkin, and Ian Kerr. Cheltenham: Edward Elgar.

Keeton, R. William, and Evan Kwerel. 1984. Externalities in Automobile Insurance and the Underinsured Driver Problem. *Journal of Law and Economics* 27 (1): 149–179.

Koops, Bert-Jaap, Hildebrandt Mireille, and David-Oliviere Jaquet-Chiffell. 2010. Bridging the Accountability Gap: Rights for New Entities in the Information Society? *Minnesota Journal of Law, Science & Technology* 11 (2): 497–561.

Kornhauser, A. Lewis, and Richard L. Revesz. 1998. Regulation of Hazardous Wastes. In *The New Palgrave Dictionary of Economics and the Law*, ed. Peter Newman, 238–242. London: Macmillan.

Kovac, Mitja, and Rok Spruk. 2016. Institutional Development, Transaction Costs and Economic Growth: Evidence from a Cross-Country Investigation. *Journal of Institutional Economics* 12 (1): 129–159.

Kovac, Mitja, Salvini Datta, and Rok Spruk. 2020. Pharmaceutical Product Liability, Litigation Regimes and the Propensity to Patent: An Empirical Firm-Level Investigation. *SAGE Open*, 1–15. https://doi.org/10.31124/advance.12136155.v1.

Kraakman, H. Reimer. 2000. Vicarious and Corporate Civil Liability. In *Encyclopaedia of Law and Economics*, ed. Gerrit De Geest and Boudewijn Bouckaert, Vol. II. Civil Law and Economics. Cheltenham: Edward Elgar.

Logue, D. Kyle. 1994. Solving the Judgement-proof Problem. *Texas Law Review* 72: 1375–1394.

Luppi, Barbara, and Francesco Parisi. 2009. Optimal Timing of Legal Intervention: The Role of Timing Rules. *Harvard Law Review* 122 (2): 18–31.

MacKaay, Ejan. 2015. *Law and Economics for Civil Law Systems*. Cheltenham: Edward Elgar.

Malott, W. Richard. 1988. Rule-Governed Behaviour and Behavioural Anthropology. *Behavioural Analysis* 11 (2): 181–203.

Manning, F. John. 1997. Textualism as a Nondelegation Doctrine. *Columbia Law Review* 97 (2): 673–685.

McGuire, B. Jean. 1988. A Dialectical Analysis of Interorganizational Networks. *Journal of Management* 14 (1): 109–124.

Menell, S. Peter. 1998. Regulation of Toxic Substances. In *The New Palgrave Dictionary of Economics and the Law*, ed. Peter Newman, 255–263. London: Macmillan.

Metz, Cade. 2018. As China Marches Forward on AI, the White House Is Silent. *New York Times*.

North, C. Douglas. 1981. *Structure and Change in Economic History*. New York: Norton & Company.

North, C. Douglas, and Richard P. Thomas. 1973. *The Rise of the Western World: A New Economic History*. New York: Cambridge University Press.

Pagallo, Ugo. 2013. *The Laws of Robots: Crimes, Contracts and Torts*. New York: Springer.

Parisi, Francesco, and Nita Ghei. 2007. Legislative Today or Wait Until Tomorrow? An Investment Approach to Lawmaking. In *Legal Orderings and Economics Institutions*, ed. Fabrizio Caffagi, Antonio Nicita, and Ugo Pagano. London: Routledge.

Pitchford, Rohan. 1995. How Liable Should a Lender Be? The Case of Judgement-Proof Firms and Environmental Risk. *American Economic Review* 85: 1171–1186.

Pitchford, Rohan. 1998. Judgement-Proofness. In *The New Palgrave Dictionary of Economics and the Law*, ed. Peter Newman Peter, 380–383. London: Macmillan.

Pindyck, S. Robert. 1991. Irreversibility, Uncertainty and Investment. *Journal of Economic Literature* 29 (3): 1110–1148.

Posner, A. Richard. 2014. *Economic Analysis of Law*, 9th ed. New York: Wolters Kluwer.

Ringe, Wolf-Georg, and Christopher Ruof. 2020. Regulating Fintech in the EU: The Case for a Guided Sandbox. *European Journal of Risk Regulation*. https://doi.org/10.1017/err.2020.8.

Ringleb, H. Al, and Steven N. Wiggins. 1990. Liability and Large-Scale, Long-Ter, Hazards. *Journal of Political Economy* 98: 574–595.

Rose-Ackerman, Susan. 1991a. Tort Law as a Regulatory System. *AEA Papers and Proceedings* 81 (2): 54–58.

Rose-Ackerman, Susan. 1991b. Regulation and the Law of Torts. *American Economic Review* 81 (2): 54–58.

Russell, Stuart. 2019. *Human Compatible: AI and the Problem of Control*. London: Allen Lane.

Schäfer, Hans-Bernd, and Claus Ott. 2004. *The Economic Analysis of Civil Law*. Cheltenham: Edward Elgar.

Schmitz, W. Patrick. 2000. On the Joint Use of Liability and Safety Regulation. *International Review of Law and Economics* 20 (1): 371–382.

Shavell, M. Steven. 1984. Liability for Harm Versus Regulation of Safety. *Journal of Legal Studies* 13 (2): 357–374.

Shavell, Steven. 1986. The Judgment Proof Problem. *International Review of Law and Economics* 6 (1): 45–58.

Shavell, M. Steven. 2004. *Foundations of the Economics Analysis of Law*. Cambridge: Harvard University Press.

Shavell, M. Steven. 2007. Liability for Accidents. In *Handbook of Law and Economics*, Vol. 1, ed. Mitchell A. Polinsky and Steven Shavell, 139–183. Amsterdam: North-Holland.

Smith, W. George, and Charles Anthon. 1858. *A Dictionary of Greek and Roman Antiquities*. London: Harper.

Solum, B. Lawrence. 1992. Legal Personhood for Artificial Intelligences. *North Carolina Law Review* 70: 1231.

Sykes, Alan. 1984. The Economics of Vicarious Liability. *Yale Law Journal* 93: 168–206.

Taleb, N. Nicholas. 2012. *Anti-fragile: Things That Gain from Disorder*. London: Penguin Books.

Terré, Francois, Philippe Simler, and Yves Lequette. 2009. *Droit Civil: Les Obligations*, 10th ed. Paris: Deloz.

Teubner, Gunther. 2007. Rights of Non-humans? Electronic Agents and Animals as New Actors in Politics and Law. Lecture delivered 17 January 2007, Max Weber Lecture Series MWP 2007/04.

Thomas, A.C. Joseph. 1976. *Textbook on Roman Law*. Amsterdam: North-Holland.

Tinbergen, Jan. 1952. *On the Theory of Economic Policy*. Amsterdam: North-Holland.

Turner, Jacob. 2019. *Robot Rules: Regulating Artificial Intelligence*. Cham: Palgrave Macmillan.

Veljanovski, G. Cento. 1982. The Employment and Safety Effects of Employers' Liability. *Scottish Journal of Political Economy* 29 (3): 256–271.

Viscusi, W. Kip, and Michael J. Moore. 1993. Product Liability, Research and Development, and Innovation. *Journal of Political Economy* 101 (1): 161–184.

Wright, R. George. 2001. The Pale Cast of Thought: On the Legal Status of Sophisticated Androids. *Legal Studies Forum* 25 (3 & 4): 297–314.

Yordanova, Katerina. 2019. The Shifting Sands of Regulatory Sandboxes for AI. KU Leuven Research Paper.

Zetzsche, A. Dirk, Ross P. Buckley, Janos N. Barberis, and Douglas W. Arner. 2017–2018. Regulating a Revolution: From Regulatory Sandboxes to Smart Regulation. *Fordham Journal Corporate & Financial Law* 23 (1): 31–103.

Zimmermann, Reinhard. 2001. *Roman Law, Contemporary Law, European Law: The Civilian Tradition Today*. Oxford: Oxford University Press.

Zweigert, Konrad, and Hein Kötz. 1998. *Introduction to Comparative Law*, 3rd ed. Oxford: Clarendon Press.

Epilogue

Alan Turing, one of the founding fathers of artificial intelligence has contemplated the scenario in which a machine thinks and thinks more intelligently than we do also considered the long-term future and potential consequences of AI for humanity. In Hollywood movies and science-fiction novels set in the far future humanity barely survives a biblical war with the super-intelligent machines and the mere prospect of such a super-human intelligence does make us all uneasy. Could such super-intelligent machines subjugate or eliminate the human race? If this is a realistic scenario then the regulatory response is more than clear. Lawmakers around the world should according to the optimal-design timing immediately ban the development and deployment of super-intelligent AI agents. However, no one can actually predict when real super-intelligent human-level AI agents will arrive, yet our experience with other technological breakthroughs suggests that it would be prudent to assume that progress could occur quite quickly and thus we have to prepare accordingly.

This book has argued that artificial intelligence is actually unlike any other technological inventions created by humans and its judgement-proofness feature may severely undermine the human liability-related preventive function of the current tort law systems. Undoubtedly AI technology will bring benefits, but the identified judgement-proof characteristic of super-intelligent AI agent calls for an urgent regulatory action. Current reliance on the existing *ex post* liability-related law of torts might be ill-considered and could result in unprecedented hazards

M. Kovač, *Judgement-Proof Robots and Artificial Intelligence*,
https://doi.org/10.1007/978-3-030-53644-2

and subjugation of the human race. Employed classic comparative law and economics methodology shows that evolution of a super-intelligent AI and its capacity to develop characteristics and even personhood (and consequently also completely unexpected harmful consequences) never envisaged by its designer or producer undermines the effectiveness of the classical strict liability and other tort law instruments. Deterrence goal is corrupted irrespective of the liability rule since the judgement-proof AI will not internalize costs of the accident that they might cause. Moreover, judgement-proof characteristic of the autonomous AI also implies that AI's activity levels will tend to be socially excessive and they will contribute to the excessive risk-taking. Since, as comparative law and economics analysis suggests tortious liability (of any kind) will not furnish adequate incentives to alleviate the risk the question of effective dealing with such a super-intelligent AI agents boils down to the efficient ex ante regulatory intervention.

This book has identified the judgement-proofness of super-intelligent AI agents and has contemplated on how to regulate such judgement-proof problem, on who should be responsible for harms caused by super-intelligent AI and how to effectively deter, prevent the worst-case scenario of unprecedented hazards and even of potential subjugation or elimination of the human race. My intention was not to write exact rules but instead to provide a comparative law and economics blueprint for lawmakers around the world capable of making such rules. To end, there is an attempt at an anti-fragile view of the law and its persistent, robust responses to uncontemplated technological shocks and related hazards. Namely, the law might be much more resilient in dealing with technological innovation and related hazards then it is often believed. This feature of the legal system in allowing it to deal with the unknown is beyond resilience and robustness, since every technological shock in the last millennium made the legal system even better.

Justice Benjamin Cardozo in his famous book on the nature of judicial process from 1921 observed that ever in the making, as the law develops through the centuries, is this new faith which silently and steadily effaces our mistakes and eccentricities. In his words, the future takes care of such things. In the endless process of testing and retesting, there is a constant rejection of the dross, and a constant retention of whatever is pure and sound and fine.

Human evolution from the earliest times on reads as a constant sequence of technological-institutional innovations and progress.

However, in the recorded human history we have never ever been able to create something that surpasses our own intelligence. This time the trajectory suggests that we might succeed! Our ultimate and maybe indeed the final innovation would be the outsourcing of our biggest comparative advantage that we possess—our human intelligence. This threat is non-trivial and eminent. Thus, the time has ripe for lawyers to step in and to prevent this worst-case scenario of human subjugation and potential extinction.

Index

M. Kovač, *Judgement-Proof Robots and Artificial Intelligence*, https://doi.org/10.1007/978-3-030-53644-2

The manufacturer's authorised representative in the EU is Springer
Nature Customer Service Centre GmbH, Europaplatz 3, 69115 Heidelberg,
Germany. If you have any concerns regarding our products, please
contact ProductSafety@springernature.com

Printed and bound by CPI Group (UK) Ltd, Croydon, CR0 4YY
30/09/2026
02225514-0012